An
Introduction to
subject indexing

An Introduction to subject indexing

Second edition

A G BROWN

in collaboration with
D W LANGRIDGE AND J MILLS

CLIVE BINGLEY LONDON

First published in 1976 in two volumes
This second edition first published 1982
by Clive Bingley Ltd, 16 Pembridge Road, London W11 3HL
Set in 10 on 11 point Press Roman by Allset
Printed and bound in the UK by
Redwood Burn Ltd, Trowbridge
Copyright © A G Brown 1982
ISBN: 0-85157-331-2

British Library Cataloguing in Publication Data

Brown, A G
    Introduction to subject indexing. — 2nd ed.
    1. Subject cataloguing — Programmed instruction
    2. Classification — Programmed instruction
    I. Title   II. Langridge, D W   III. Mills, J
    025.4'7   Z695

ISBN 0-85157-331-2

CONTENTS

Preface

Appendix

Index

PREFACE TO THE SECOND EDITION

This book was first published in two volumes in 1976. It was developed from work initially carried out under a research project, funded by the then Office for Scientific and Technical Information, designed to investigate the applicability of programmed instruction techniques in the teaching of practical subject indexing. This project was conducted at the School of Librarianship, the Polytechnic of North London with cooperation from the College of Librarianship Wales.

Many programmed texts in the field of subject indexing concentrate upon the translation stage of indexing aiming to impart skills in the use of particular indexing languages. As we stated in the first edition, our intention is to offer a course of instruction which attempts to present an integrated view of some of the basic principles of subject indexing, not to impart a high degree of familiarity with any particular system.

Thus we do not concern ourselves with the Colon Classification and UDC as ends in themselves but to demonstrate the use of classification schemes and the employment of the principles of subject analysis dealt with earlier in the course. In a similar vein we do not treat chain procedure in pre-coordinate index construction primarily as a practical skill to be mastered for its own sake. We believe that an understanding of this technique provides a sound basis for a wider appreciation of pre-coordinate indexing practices and of different types of pre-coordinate indexes.

In this second edition the existing text has been re-structured into one volume. To this we have added a section dealing with the fundamental characteristics of post-coordinate indexing which builds upon the concepts covered earlier.

Rapid developments have taken place over recent years in the field of subject indexing, notably in the sphere of computer applications. The situation now facing the entrant into the areas of library and information work is one of diversity and change. These characteristics are likely to intensify. We feel that it is now probably more important than ever that the beginner is made aware of basic principles which underly this diversity. It is with such principles that this course attempts to deal in the hope that the reader will be better prepared to encounter indexing and retrieval practices lying outside its particular scope.

A G BROWN
School of Library, Archive and Information Studies
University College London
July 1981

SECTION 1: INTRODUCTION TO SUBJECT INDEXING

The principal function of any library is to make the information it contains available to the library users at their request. In order to fulfil this function, the information which is stored in the library must be recovered, or retrieved, from the store. The process of recovering or retrieving information is called, quite simply, *INFORMATION RETRIEVAL.*

INDEXING is once of the activities—the major one, in fact,—which supports the process of information retrieval.

In this course we are concerned with that very important part of indexing called *SUBJECT INDEXING.*

In particular, the aim of the course is to teach some of the *practical* skills required in subject indexing, ie some of the techniques of *PRACTICAL SUBJECT INDEXING.*

In order that you should be able to perform these required skills with greater understanding, and therefore with greater competence, selected elements of the theory of subject indexing will be included.

This course is not presented in the form of a conventional textbook, and in most cases you will not read the pages consecutively. Most pages are divided into individually numbered frames. On many pages you will be asked a question. The answer you give or select will direct you to the next frame you should read. In this way, the material is adjusted to your own particular requirements.

For example, having read the above paragraphs, what is the aim of this course?

To teach the complete theory and practice of
subject indexing   – frame 6
To teach some of the theory and practice of
subject indexing   – frame 4

---

2 (12)
No, this is an incorrect answer. If the library catalogue contained only *one* substitute for each document and arranged these in the *same* sequence as the shelf order for documents, it would simply duplicate shelf order. This duplicate order would have the same inherent limitations as the shelf arrangement of documents.

Return to frame 12. When you have re-read the frame, select the correct answer and proceed with the course

3 (5)

Your answer: a library fulfils its function of information retrieval by maintaining some system for the recovery of documents from its collection. Quite right.

No matter how *large* the collection, the library is of little value if it is unable to retrieve the right documents as and when they are reuqired. To do this it must maintain an *information retrieval system.*

When documents relevant to a request have been located, a *MATCH* has been achieved between the information requested and the information retrieved.

In other words, the *information supplied* in the document, or documents, *MATCHES*, to an acceptable degree, the *information demanded* by the user.

To achieve a successful match is the central objective of information retrieval.

In relation to a given request for information, under what conditions can this objective be considered successfully achieved?

If relevant documents are contained in the collection   – frame 22

If relevant documents are located in the collection   – frame 9

---

4 (1, 6)

(NB: Numbers given in brackets refer to frames which have led to the one you are reading. This is to help you retrace your steps if necessary.)
You are correct in your answer. The aim of the course is to teach you only *some* of the theory and practices of subject indexing.

In particular, our concern is with the problems of the subject indexing of a given document in a given library system. We shall begin by defining two frequently recurring terms—library and document.

There are many kinds of library and information centre each fulfilling their individual purposes. The public library, the university library, the library of a commercial firm, for example, each serve the various needs of differing groups of users.

The fundamental characteristic common to *all* libraries is that they are stores of information.

This information is contained in information carriers, which vary widely in their physical forms, eg books, films or gramophone records.

In this course we are concerned not with any particular kind of library nor with any particular form of information carrier. We shall thus use the terms

DOCUMENT to mean any form of information carrier
and

LIBRARY to mean any collection of documents
Continue on the next frame.

5 (4)

A library acquires documents because they contain information of the kind that is likely to be of interest to its users. At this stage we need not worry about the precise nature of this information.

Information retrieval is the process of satisfying the requests of library users by providing them with relevant information contained within the library. It is the principal function of a library.

The term information retrieval usually implies *document retrieval.* That is, the satisfaction of a request for information by retrieving a document, or documents, which will contain information relevant to that request.

As such it is usually distinguished from *DATA RETRIEVAL*—the satisfaction of a request for information by providing the information as a direct answer to the question.

We shall use the following definition of *INFORMATION RETRIEVAL: The recovery of documents from a given collection which are relevant to a request.*

By what means does a library fulfil its function of information retrieval?

By acquiring a large collection of documents — frame 13

By maintaining some system for the recovery of documents from its collection — frame 3

---

6 (1)

(NB: Numbers given in brackets refer to frames which have led to the one you are reading. This is to help you retrace your steps if necessary.)

No, this is not quite correct. To attempt to teach you the *complete* theory and practice of subject indexing is beyond the scope of this course.

We shall concentrate on only some of the skills required in practical subject indexing.

Moreover, it was stated that only selected elements of subject indexing will be included. Those elements which will contribute directly to the execution of these skills with greater competence.

Proceed to frame 4 and continue with the course. Remember to read each frame *very carefully.*

7 (10)

Your answer: only set A constitutes a class of documents. No, this is not correct.

You are right in thinking that set A constitutes a class. All the documents in this class share at least one characteristic in common—they are all *about* the French Revolution. Their common characteristic is their *subject content.*

However, there is also a common characteristic possessed by the documents in the other two sets. Your answer does not go far enough.

Read frame 10 once more and reconsider the question.

---

8 (10)

You say that only sets A and B constitute classes of documents. This is not true.

You have correctly observed that all the documents in set A are about the same subject, and all the documents in set B are written by the same author. These are therefore two classes of documents defined respectively by the common characteristics of subject content and authorship.

But what about set C? All the documents in this set are published by the same publisher, the Cambridge University Press. This is also a class of documents for each document possesses at least one characteristic in common—its publisher.

We said that, in information retrieval, a class is a set of documents which share *some* property or characteristic in common.

Your answer should have been: *all* the sets constitute classes.

Go to frame 14, and continue with the course.

Your answer: If relevant documents are located in the collection. Yes, you are correct in saying that only under this condition has a match been successfully achieved.

The possession of relevant documents, does not, itself, imply a match in terms of information retrieval. To achieve a match we must be able to locate these documents within the collection.

In order to locate documents relevant to a request, the collection, that is the information store, must be examined or *SEARCHED*.

To illustrate the process of searching let us take a simple example of practical information retrieval. Suppose you wish to borrow a book from your public library about '*Programmed instruction*'.

Now the collection of documents in the public library covers the whole range of knowledge. In the attempt to satisfy your particular request for information, you would not expect to have to examine every document in that collection. You would not expect to search the entire information store.

You would ignore the documents about history, engineering, bio-chemistry etc. You would confine your search to those documents about '*Programmed instruction*'. Within this group of documents, probably shelved with other documents about education, you would most likely find one or more relevant to your needs. At this point you would have achieved a *match* between information demanded and information supplied.

It is obviously impracticable to search the entire information store in the satisfaction of a particular request for information.

The basic principle of information retrieval is to search only a limited part of the store in response to each request, that part which is potentially relevant to the request.

In the above instance, your request was for information about a particular subject, '*Programmed instruction*'. You would therefore limit your search to that part of the store potentially relevant to this subject.

A limited part of the store, such as this, is an example of a *CLASS*. Continue on the next frame.

A CLASS IS A SET OF THINGS WHICH SHARE SOME PROPERTY, OR CHARACTERISTIC, IN COMMON.

For example, violins, cellos, harps and guitars are all musical instruments which produce sound through the bowing or plucking of strings. This particular medium of sound production is a characteristic which they all possess, it is a *common characteristic*.

We can thus say that violins, cellos, harps and guitars form a part of that *class* of musical instruments called *stringed instruments*.

Other classes of musical instruments defined by the characteristic of sound production would be percussion instruments, wind instruments, etc.

In information retrieval, a class is a *set of documents* which share some property or characteristic in common.

For example, the set of documents about '*Programmed instruction*' forms a class by virtue of sharing the common characteristic of *subject content*. Each document is about '*Programmed instruction*'.

Look at the following set of documents.

A A set of documents about the French Revolution
B A set of documents written by Thomas Carlyle
C A set of documents published by the Cambridge University Press

Which of the following statements is true of these sets

Only A constitutes a class   — frame 7
Only A and B constitute a class   — frame 8
All constitute classes   — frame 14

You say the document will not be automatically retrieved. Quite right.

If '*The aims of education*' is classified by its subject content and arranged with other documents about education, it cannot at the same time be displayed as belonging to that class of documents written by A N Whitehead.

This illustrates the major weakness inherent in the shelf arrangement of documents as an aid to their retrieval.

Although a document can be usefully regarded as belonging to a number of classes, it can only be located in *one* of these.

The only way in which a library could simultaneously display a document in all its potentially relevant classes, would be to buy several copies of the document. A policy of multiple acquisition of all documents is obviously uneconomic.

There are other weaknesses in shelf arrangement for retrieval purposes:

In any given class, not all the documents belonging to that class are necessarily present at any one time, eg some on loan from the library.

In any given class, not all the documents belonging to that class can necessarily be stored in any one place in the library, eg large size books, pamphlets etc often require special storage facilities.

Continue on the next frame.

12 (11)

The physical arrangement, or 'shelf arrangement', of documents is of limited value as a tool for information retrieval. To help overcome these limitations *records* are made of the documents held in the library.

Such records come in a variety of physical forms. One commonly used form is the 5 × 3 inch catalogue card upon which the required data is typed.

Each record of a document contains a description of the document— its author, title, place of publication, publishers, date of publication etc. The record can thus act as a *SUBSTITUTE* for the document.

These document substitutes are arranged together to form a *LIBRARY CATALOGUE*. The catalogue forms a complete record of all the documents held in the library.

For each document several substitutes can be made and these can be arranged in several different sequences, or ways, in the catalogue.

The principal limitation in the shelf arrangement of documents as an aid to information retrieval is that a document can only be located in any one class at any one time.

How can the library catalogue overcome this limitation?

By containing one substitute for each document and arranging these in the same sequence as the shelf order of documents	— frame 2
By containing more than one substitute for each document and arranging these in sequences differing from shelf order	— frame 20

---

13 (5)

You think that a library will fulfil its function of information retrieval by acquiring a large collection of documents.

A large collection of documents may well contain a great deal of useful information of value to the library users. However, a large collection of documents is of little value in itself unless documents can be recovered when needed. Information retrieval is the process of recovering documents when they are required.

Read frame 5 again. Then reconsider the question and continue with the course.

14 (7, 8, 10)

You say that all the sets of documents named constitute classes of documents. You are correct.

All the documents in each set share at least *one* characteristic in common. They are all either about the same subject, written by the same author or published by the same publisher. Each of the three sets is thus a class of documents, each class being defined by a different characteristic.

CLASSIFICATION is the activity of forming classes. In the particular context of information retrieval, this activity is sometimes referred to as *LIBRARY* or *BIBLIOGRAPHIC CLASSIFICATION.*

At its widest interpretation, the classification of documents can be taken to mean the definition of classes by any of a number of possible characteristics. In this broad sense it is the basic activity in all aspects of information retrieval.

Continue on the next frame

15 (14)

The whole process of information retrieval is initiated by a request for information.

Now these requests are couched in a variety of ways which express differing approaches to information needs.

For example, there are requests for information on *named subjects*. 'What has the library got *on programmed instruction*', 'Have you any books *about classification*?' etc.

There are requests for a document, or documents by a *named author* or from a *named publisher*.

These kinds of requests, and many others, all exhibit valid approaches to the expression of information needs by library users.

You have seen that the basic principle in information retrieval is to search only a limited part of the store in response to each request. That part of the store which is potentially relevant to that request.

In other words, we search that *class of documents* which is potentially relevant to the request.

It is obviously useful to have the documents themselves arranged into classes. The searcher can then to to the library shelves and examine the relevant class.

If you wish to retrieve a document about a named subject it would be useful to have the documents arranged in classes defined by their subject content. We presumed this principle of organization in the case of searching the public library for a document about programmed instruction.

If you wanted to retrieve a document by a named author, it would be useful to have the documents arranged in a classified order defined by their authorship.

In fact, it would be useful to have the documents arranged into classes defined by all the characteristics by which they are sought.
Continue on the next frame

---

16 (15)

So far, so good. Now take the case of an individual document, say '*The aims of education*' by A N Whitehead.

This document is relevant to a request for information about education. It is also relevant to a request for documents written by A N Whitehead.

Suppose the library possesses only one copy of this document and it has been arranged on the shelves along with other documents about education. It has been arranged in a class defined by its subject content.

A request is placed for documents by A N Whitehead. What will be the result if the library relies on shelf arrangement as the sole aid to its information retrieval?

The document will be automatically retrieved   – frame 24
The document will not be automatically retrieved   – frame 11

You say that the heading on each document entry will consist of a description of a *class* to which the document belongs, rather than a full description of the *document.* Yes, you are right.

Take, for example, the document '*Elements of library classification*' by S R Ranganathan.

Let us say that this document can usefully be regarded as belonging to two classes—one defined by its *authorship*, one by its *subject content.*

It will thus receive two entries in the catalogue—one having an *AUTHOR HEADING*, one a *SUBJECT HEADING.*

These entries could be arranged in a card catalogue in a single alphabetical sequence as illustrated below.

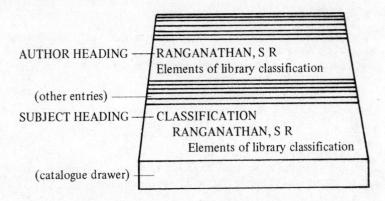

On searching the catalogue for information on *classification*, this document will be indicated as relevant.

On searching for documents written by *S R Ranganathan*, this document will also be indicated as relevant.

Because the catalogue can contain more than one substitute for each document it is said to allow for *MULTIPLE ACCESS* to documents—ie access via all the different characteristics by which a document is liable to be sought and which define its class membership.

Later in this course we shall have much more to say about library catalogues, their structure and function.

Continue on the next frame

18 (17)

For the present it is sufficient to note that, as aids to the retrieval of documents, they have the following advantages over shelf arrangement:

1 They allow for the multiple access to documents.

2 In any given class, all the documents contained within that class can be represented at one place in the catalogue, irrespective of their shelf location in the library.

3 At any given time, all the documents in a class will be represented in the catalogue as being contained within that class, even if they may be temporarily removed from the library eg on loan.

Continue on the next frame

---

19 (18)

By means of the arrangement of document substitutes in library catalogues, and also by the arrangement of documents themselves, it is possible to point out, or indicate, classes of documents. In doing this we facilitate the process of information retrieval.

In the context of information retrieval, an *INDEX* is some kind of physical mechanism, or tool, which serves to indicate to the searcher those parts of an information store which are potentially relevant to a request.

A library catalogue is a form of index.

Would it be true to say that the shelf arrangement of documents is also a kind of index according to our definition of the term?

Yes   — frame 25
No   — frame 21

---

20 (12)

Your answer: by containing more than one substitute for each document and arranging these in sequences differing from shelf order.

Correct. It is by this means that the library catalogue can overcome the limitation of one document, one location which is inherent in shelf arrangement.

Document substitutes eg catalogue cards, are relatively cheap to produce. It is therefore quite feasible to have several such substitutes for each document. Given this condition, each document can be displayed simultaneously in a number of classes via the medium of these substitutes arranged in the catalogue.

Each document substitute is said to constitute an *ENTRY* for that document in the catalogue.

Each document entry serves to indicate the inclusion of that document within a class of documents and so facilitates its retrieval.

The entries are arranged, and therefore sought, in the catalogue according to their *HEADINGS*. So called because they are typed at the top or 'head' of the catalogue cards.

What will the heading for a document entry consist of?

A full description of the document	— frame 23
A description of a class to which the document belongs	— frame 17

---

21 (19)

Your answer is incorrect. The shelf arrangement of documents is definitely a kind of index according to our definition of the term, just as a library catalogue is.

They are both mechanisms by which it is possible to indicate classes of documents and therefore those parts of an information store potentially relevant to a request.

Return to frame 19 and consider the definition of an index again. Then reconsider the question and proceed with the course.

---

22 (3)

You say that a match can be considered successfully achieved if documents relevant to a request are *contained* in the collection.

No, this is not, strictly speaking, a sufficient condition. The fact that relevant documents are contained somewhere in the collection does not mean that these documents have been *located* in that collection.

Return to frame 3 and read the paragraphs on matching again. Then reconsider your answer and proceed with the course.

---

23 (20)

You say that the heading on each document entry will consist of a *full description of the document*. This is not so.

Entries are arranged, and therefore sought, in the catalogue according to their headings. As the purpose of each entry is to indicate the class membership of a document and, by doing so, facilitate its retrieval, a full description of the documents would not necessarily fulfil the function of a heading.

Return to frame 20 and read again the paragraphs on document substitutes. Then select the correct answer and proceed.

24 (16)

You say that the document will be automatically retrieved. No, you are wrong.

The library possesses only *one* copy of this document and arranges it with other documents about education. It cannot then be located in the class defined by its authorship. It is, however, this class that we should search if the request is for documents written by A N Whitehead.

Return to frame 16 and then reconsider the question.

---

25 (19)

You consider that the shelf arrangement of documents and the library catalogue are *both* forms of indexes. Yes, this is correct.

They both serve to indicate classes of documents. Each class of documents thus indicated constitutes a limited part of the information store which may be potentially relevant to a request. By this means they both facilitate the searching for, and retrieval of, a document.

The library catalogue is, of course, a much more effective index to the documents in the collection than the arrangement of the documents themselves.

There are also indexes which are not necessarily confined to the documents in a particular library. Such an index is generally distinguished by the term *BIBLIOGRAPHY*.

The limitations placed upon the documents indexed in a bibliography might be, for example, place or date of publication, or subject content rather than possession by a particular library.

The principles employed in the construction of bibliographies are the same as in the construction of library catalogues.

From now on we will refer to library catalogues simply as *catalogues*. We will use the term *index* to imply some form of *catalogue* or *bibliography*.

Continue on the next frame

At this point we can attempt a definition of the activity of *INDEXING*, and, more particularly, of *SUBJECT INDEXING*. This will give you a general idea of the principles and practices which you will go on to examine in greater detail in the succeeding sections of this course.

In the literature of librarianship the term *INDEXING* is used with several shades of meaning. We use it to cover all activities involved in the construction of indexes. As such, it is the major activity supporting *all* aspects of information retrieval.

As you have seen, the process of information retrieval is initiated by requests in which information needs are expressed in a variety of ways, eg a document, or documents, by a specified author, or about a specified subject.

In this course we are particularly interested in that aspect of indexing which supports the retrieval of documents in response to requests for information about a *named subject*. This is the aspect called *SUBJECT INDEXING*.

SUBJECT INDEXING thus involves:

1 The classification of documents on the basis of their subject content. In the context of information retrieval, the term classification is used almost exclusively in this restricted sense and will be so used from now on in this course.

2 The construction of indexes which facilitate the retrieval of documents on the basis of their subject content.

There must be one final note. Subject indexing possesses its own body of theory. The title of this course is *PRACTICAL SUBJECT INDEXING*, that is, the practical procedures involved in the subject indexing of a given document for a given retrieval system.

This course will only include those aspects of subject indexing theory which are deemed to contribute directly to the effective execution of these procedures.

Continue on the next frame

27

The following sequence of frames provides you with a review of some of the important points made in this first section of the course.

This review is designed to help you check your understanding of these points.

The frames are to be read consecutively, but in each frame an important word is omitted from the text and provided below the frame.

As you read each frame, cover the area below each frame and attempt to supply the missing word. Then check that your response is correct before proceeding.

Continue on the next frame

28

Information retrieval is the process of recovering information, relevant to a request, from a library or information store. This usually implies the recovery of relevant documents.

Information retrieval is the principal function of a library.

In order to fulfil this function, the library must maintain a system for the _____ of documents.

RECOVERY or RETRIEVAL
Continue on the next frame

29

In order to retrieve documents in response to a request for information the store must be searched.

When this search results in the recovery of relevant documents, it is said that a _____ has been achieved between information demanded and information supplied.

MATCH
Continue on the next frame

30

It is not a feasible proposition to search the entire store in response to each request.

A central principle in information retrieval is to search only a limited part of the store in the attempt to satisfy each request, that part of the store which is potentially _____ to the request.

RELEVANT
Continue on the next frame

31

These potentially relevant parts of the store searched are examples of classes.

A class is a set of things which share some property or characteristic in common.

In information retrieval, a class is a set of _____ which share some property or characteristic in common.

DOCUMENTS
Continue on the next frame

32

A single document can be regarded as belonging to several classes each defined by a different characteristic which it possesses and by which it might be requested and sought, eg its author or its subject content.

The shelf location of a document will indicate its membership of only one _____ .

CLASS
Continue on the next frame

33

To help overcome this principal limitation of the shelf arrangement of documents as an aid to their retrieval, we make records of the documents possessed by the library.

These records are arranged together to form the library _____.

CATALOGUE
Continue on the next frame

34

The shelf arrangement of documents and the library catalogue both aid information retrieval by indicating potentially relevant classes of documents.

They are both forms of _____.

INDEXES
Continue on the next frame

35

Indexing, which includes the construction of indexes, is the major activity supporting all aspects of information retrieval.

We are primarily interested in one aspect of information retrieval; the retrieval of documents relevant to a request for information about a named _____ .

SUBJECT

Continue on the next frame

36

That aspect of indexing which supports the retrieval of documents about a named subject is called subject indexing.

Subject indexing involves

1 The classification of documents on the basis of their _____ .
2 The construction of _____ which help the retrieval of documents about named subjects.

1 SUBJECT CONTENT
2 INDEXES

If you are dissatisfied with your responses, go back and revise such parts of the text as you think fit.

If you are satisfied with your responses, proceed to section 2 of the course, frame 37.

SECTION 2: SUBJECT ANALYSIS/PART 1

It has been established that subject indexing facilitates the retrieval of documents that are relevant to a request for information on a particular subject.

In the subject indexing of a document we indicate its subject content— what it is about. We provide an *index description* of the document, ie a very brief description of its subject content.

The first problem in practical subject indexing is to decide exactly what the document is about.

This problem is not always as simple as it might appear. It involves the *SUBJECT ANALYSIS* of the document.

In this section of the course we shall be concerned with the techniques and implications of subject analysis and, therefore, the nature of the subject content of documents.

The subject analysis of a document exerts a controlling influence on *all* the subsequent steps involved in its subject indexing. It is, therefore, essential to work accurately and consistently at this most important primary stage.

To save unnecessary repetition of the word 'subject' we shall from now on refer to subject indexing simply as 'indexing', acknowledging the fact that we are using the term in this restricted sense.

Continue on the next frame

As the indexer is concerned with the subject content of documents, he is obviously concerned with knowledge. When indexing a document it is clearly essential to understand, at least in very general terms, what the document is *about.*

This does not mean that the indexer must be expert in all areas of knowledge, that is in the whole *'universe of knowledge'*.

However, the study of the universe of knowledge, in respect of the nature, structure and interrelationships of areas of knowledge, is a very useful and valid background study to indexing. As a background study, it is beyond the scope of this course.

Subject analysis does *not* mean the analysis of subjects, or areas of knowledge, in this broad sense.

Subject analysis means the analysis of the subject content of individual documents, that is, *the analysis of subjects as they are expressed in documents.*

Take, for example, that area of knowledge called geography. The analysis of geography, its nature, structure, methodology, and relationships with other areas of knowledge, such as economics, geology, biology and history, would form a part of the background study to indexing—the study of the universe of knowledge.

In subject analysis we are more particularly concerned with the analysis of geography as it is expressed in documents.

We are likely to be concerned with the analysis of such subjects as
'The development of medieval field patterns in England'
or
'The geography of chalk downlands'

Subject analysis could be said to be the analysis of 'documentary subjects' rather than the analysis of subjects, or knowledge, in any more abstract sense.

Continue on the next frame

---

39 (38)

The seeking of information on subjects is often embodied in requests for
named documents
eg 'Do you have 'English field systems' by H L Gray?'

But it is also frequently the case that information on subjects is sought in such requests as,
eg 'Has the library got any books on English medieval field systems?'

Although both the above requests are for information about a particular *subject*, the first is stated obliquely and can be met relatively easily by, in this case, an *author* or *title catalogue*.

The second request is stated directly, ie the information sought is named as a subject, 'English medieval field systems'. It is this approach which is usually thought of as being the 'subject approach' to information—only the name of the *subject*, on which information is being sought, is provided in the request.

As we are concerned with indexing which provides for the 'subject approach' to information, the indexer must attempt to anticipate the information needs of the library user at the stage of the subject analysis of a document. He must ask himself 'For what requested information would it be reasonable to expect this document to be retrieved?'

Subject analysis thus selects and names subject concepts as they are expressed, and sought, in documents.

Continue on the next frame

The subject content of a document comprises a number of concepts or ideas.

For example, a textbook on *'Social anthropology'* will contain information on a large number of concepts such as social structure, kinship, marriage, ritual etc.

In his subject analysis of a document, the indexer selects those concepts which will be used in the index description of the document for the purposes of its identification and retrieval in response to requests for information.

In producing this subject, or conceptual, analysis the indexer *names* the selected concepts in whatever words, or terms, he chooses. These may be either his own words or those used by the author of the document.

At a later stage in indexing the document, the concepts thus expressed in the subject analysis will need to be expressed in the terms of a particular 'language' used for index description.

What is the indexer's *first* job in indexing a document?

Expressing concepts or ideas selected from the
document in any convenient terms.   – frame 47
Expressing concepts or ideas selected from the
document in the terms of a particular 'language'
used for index descriptions.   – frame 44

You think that representing the dominant theme of a document by a few terms is characteristic of depth indexing.

Not so; depth indexing attempts to index a document by *all* the important concepts with which it deals.

In depth indexing we employ a high degree of exhaustivity.

This will involve a relatively *large* number of terms. Many of these terms represent concepts which, although dealt with in detail in the document, would not necessarily form a part of a brief description of its dominant theme.

Now turn to frame 51 and continue with the course.

No. Summarization does *not* attempt to list *all* the important concepts mentioned in the document.

In summarization we are concerned with stating the *total content* of the document in a brief description. We are concentrating, if you like, on the *dominant theme* of the document.

We said that the textbook on '*Social anthropology*' would be summarized as,

Social anthropology

Individual concepts such as marriage, kinship and ritual, although dealt with in the document, are not *explicitly* stated in its summarization. They are considered to be *implicit* in the general expression *Social anthropology* ie in the summarization of the total subject of the document. Now turn to frame 56 and continue with the course.

You think that this subject analysis represents the policy of depth indexing.

No, this is incorrect. You are confusing depth indexing with summarization.

If our subject analysis of the document '*British history in the nineteenth century*' represented the policy of depth indexing it would include *all* the important concepts dealt with in the document. It would include such terms as,

Great Britain/Parliamentary reform/Corn laws/Chartism/
Nineteenth century/etc

Now try another example. Suppose you have to index the document '*A social geography of Western Europe*'.

This document contains information on such concepts as settlement, urban growth, field patterns, forest clearance and many others.

Your subject analysis is

Geography/Social/Western Europe

Which indexing policy are you following?

Depth indexing   — frame 54
Summarization   — frame 46

44 (40)

No, this is not the case.

Expressing concepts, or ideas, selected from the document in any convenient terms is the *first* task of the indexer.

The expression of these selected concepts in the terms of a particular indexing language, for example a classification scheme, constitutes a subsequent stage in the indexing of a document.

This later stage is called *translation* into an indexing language.

You cannot translate concepts until you have first identified them.

In subject analysis, the indexer is free to use any words or terms he chooses to identify concepts contained in a document.

Go on to frame 47 and continue with the course.

---

45 (53)

No, you are wrong. The relationship you have chosen concerns activities and their agents. Teaching is an activity of which teachers are the agents, just as nursing is an activity of which nurses are the agents. Activities and persons cannot be in genus/species relationship.

The genus/species relationship refers only to kinds of things.

Now try again.

Which of the following would be considered a genus/species relationship in indexing?

Librarians and university librarians   — frame 49

Librarians and librarianship   — frame 55

---

46 (43)

You say you are following a policy of summarization. Quite right.

The subject analysis states the total content of the document in the brief description,

Geography/Social/Western Europe.

If you had included individual concepts, constituting sub-themes within the document, eg settlement, urban growth, field patterns, your analysis would have been representative of the policy of depth indexing.

Go to frame 53 and continue with the course.

47 (40)

You say that expressing concepts, or ideas, selected from the document in convenient terms is the indexer's *first* job in the indexing of a document. Correct.

These 'convenient' terms used in a subject analysis, may be either those of the indexer or the author of the document.

The problem of expressing the selected concepts, so named, in the terms of a particular 'language' used for index descriptions—an 'indexing language'—occurs at a later stage in indexing and will be dealt with later in this course.

Although documents contain a large number of individual subject concepts, the amount of information pertaining to each concept will vary considerably.

If a concept is recognized in the subject analysis of a document, it will form part of the eventual index description of that document. Thus, if a request is placed for information on that concept, the document will be retrieved as relevant to the request.

If a document contains very little information on a particular concept, ie the concept plays a very minor role within the document, its retrieval in response to a request for information on that concept would not be worthwhile. Therefore this concept would not be recognized in the subject analysis of the document.

At the stage of subject analysis the indexer decides which, and therefore how many, concepts are selected for indexing purposes. This decision and the resulting subject analysis is influenced by the *indexing policy* of the library.

Continue on the next frame

---

48 (47, 79)

The greater the number of concepts selected for indexing purposes, the more *EXHAUSTIVE* is the indexing.

If, in a given document, concepts A, B, C, D and E are selected for indexing purposes then the indexing of the document is more EXHAUSTIVE than if only concepts A, B and C are selected.

The number of different concepts recognized in the indexing is called the EXHAUSTIVITY of the indexing.

The degree of exhaustivity employed in indexing documents is determined by the *policy* of the library or information retrieval system.

When a high degree of exhaustivity is employed, ie when a relatively large number of concepts are indexed in each document, the policy followed is one of *DEPTH INDEXING*.

DEPTH INDEXING aims to extract all the main concepts dealt with in a document for indexing purposes.

For example, in the case of the textbook on '*Social anthropology*' the indexer, following a policy of depth indexing, would select all the main concepts present in the document—social structure, kinship, marriage, religion etc—*and name them in his subject analysis.*

Which of the following is characteristic of depth indexing?

Representing the main subject content of a
document by a few terms — frame 41
Including all the important concepts treated
in the document — frame 51

---

49 (45, 50, 53, 58, 89)

Correct. For example a professor is a kind of teacher, one who holds a chair in a university. The relationship between 'teacher' and 'professor' is therefore a genus/species relationship. So also is the relationship between 'librarian' and 'university librarian' or any other *kind* of librarian.

Another term for the genus/species relationship is the *generic relationship.*

The relationship of a species to its genus is one of *subordination.* We say that a species is on a lower *generic level* than its genus.

SPECIFICITY in indexing refers to the generic level of a concept. Thus, if we name a species in indexing we are employing a higher degree of specificity, being more *SPECIFIC*, than if we were to name its genus.

Which of the following substitutions of terms indicates a *loss* of specificity?

Using professors instead of teachers — frame 60
Using steel instead of metal — frame 62
Using cereals instead of wheat — frame 64

---

50 (53)

No, you are wrong.

The genus/species relationship refers only to the relationship existing between a thing and a kind of that thing.

The relationship between teachers and universities is not therefore a genus/species relationship. A university is not a kind of teacher.

Now try again.

Which of the following would be considered a genus/species relationship in indexing?

Librarians and university librarians — frame 49
Librarians and librarianship — frame 55

51 (41, 48, 54)
You say that including all the important concepts treated in the document is characteristic of depth indexing. This is correct.

Exactly which concepts constitute 'important' concepts will, of course, depend on the judgement of the indexer. At present it is sufficient to say that depth indexing allows for the recognition of concepts embodied not only in the *main theme* of the document but also in *sub-themes* of varying importance.

In contrast to depth indexing, *SUMMARIZATION* is the policy of recognizing only the dominant, overall theme of the document for indexing purposes.

A *SUMMARIZATION* of a document is an expression of its total content by a brief description.

Following this policy a textbook on *'Social anthropology'* would be subject analysed as, simply, Social anthropology. The individual concepts such as kinship, marriage, religion etc, ie those embodied in *sub-themes* of varying importance, are not *explicitly* stated in the summarization of the document.

Which of these definitions is correct?

Summarization lists all the important concepts mentioned in the document	— frame 42
Summarization represents the whole subject of the document	— frame 56

---

52 (56)
The subject analysis represents the indexing policy of summarization. Quite right.

The analysis states the *overall theme* of the document in the *brief description*

> History/Great Britain/Nineteenth century

If individual concepts such as parliamentary reform or Irish home rule, which constitute important sub-themes within the document, had been stated in the subject analysis it would have been representative of the policy of depth indexing.

Continue on the next frame

53 (46, 52, 55)

We must now consider the degree of *SPECIFICITY* employed in the naming of those concepts recognized in the subject analysis of a document.

In order to appreciate what is meant by the term specificity, it is necessary to look at one of the important types of *relationship* which exists between concepts. More will be said about these relationships a little later, but at present, we shall concentrate upon the *GENUS/SPECIES* relationship.

You will probably have heard of this relationship used in connection with scientific classifications of plants and animals.

In indexing we use the term to identify the relationship which exists between a *thing* and its *kinds*, ie between a *thing* and a *kind of thing*.

For example, if we say that 'building' represents a *genus*, then 'house' is a *species* of the genus building.

The relationship existing between 'building' and 'house' is a genus/species relationship, a relationship between a thing and a kind of that thing.

Again, 'university library' and 'public library' are *species* of the *genus* 'library'. They are both *kinds* of the same *thing*, ie library.

It is most important to remember that the genus/species relationship refers *only* to the relationship between a *thing and its kinds*.

It must not be confused with other types of relationship such as those between a *thing* and its *properties* or between a *thing* and an *operation*.

For example, *academic ability* is not a *kind* of student, but a *property* of students.

Which of the following would be considered a genus/species relationship in indexing?

Teaching and teachers	– frame 45
Teachers and professors	– frame 49
Teachers and universities	– frame 50

---

54 (43)

No. You have made the same mistake again.

It is most important that you clarify this idea of summarization as opposed to depth indexing.

Go back to frame 51. Read the sections on summarization and work your way through the questions again.

55 (45, 50)
No. You have just made the same mistake again.

Now return to frame 53. Read again the paragraphs explaining the genus/species relationship and try the question once more.

---

56 (42, 51)
Correct. Summarization represents the whole subject of the document.

Take another example. Suppose you have to index a document with the title *'British history in the nineteenth century'*.

This document will deal with many individual concepts. Some of the important ones would be, say, British foreign policy, parliamentary reform, Chartism, Irish home rule.

Your subject analysis of this document is,

    History/Great Britain/Nineteenth century.

Which indexing policy does this subject analysis represent?

    Depth indexing   — frame 43
    Summarization   — frame 52

---

57 (67)
No. You have repeated the same mistake.

Please return to frame 71 and read the text carefully. Then attempt the question once more.

---

58 (60, 62)
No. You have just made the same mistake twice.

Now return to frame 49 and attempt the question on loss of specificity again.

Remember that using a *broader* term indicates a *loss* of specificity.

---

59 (65)
You say you would have retrieved 10 documents. No, this is wrong.

A search of a collection very rarely, if ever, retrieves *all* the relevant documents possessed in that collection.

The recall ratio is the number of relevant documents retrieved, expressed as a proportion of the total number of relevant documents actually contained in the collection.

In our example, we assumed that *20* relevant documents were contained in the collection. If, as you say, your search retrieved only *10* of these, the recall ratio would be only $\frac{10}{20}$, or 50%. However, it was stated that the recall ratio was 75%.

Please return to frame 65. Recalculate and select the right answer.

60 (49)

No, this is incorrect. The term you have chosen indicates an *increase* in specificity, since it is one of the members of the group described by the basic term.

Professor, for example, is one kind of teacher. It is therefore a more specific term.

What you are looking for is a term that is broader and indicates a loss of specificity.

Now try again.

Using transport instead of land transport   – frame 64
Using subject indexing instead of indexing   – frame 58

---

61 (73)

You think you would have retrieved 12 relevant documents. No, you are wrong.

Now remember that precision ratio is the number of relevant documents retrieved, in proportion to the total number of documents searched and retrieved.

Let us recalculate the example.

We said that 20 documents were retrieved, but only some of these proved relevant. These relevant documents produced a precision ratio of 40%.

If 8 documents were in fact relevant, the precision ratio would be $\frac{8}{20}$ or 40%.

Your answer should therefore have been 8 relevant documents.

Please turn to frame 70 and continue with the course.

---

62 (49)

No, this is incorrect. The term you have chosen indicates an *increase* in specificity, since it is one of the members of the group described by the basic term.

Steel, for example, is one kind of metal. It is therefore a more specific term.

What you are looking for is a term that is broader and indicates a loss of specificity.

Now try again.

Using mass media instead of television   – frame 64
Using house instead of building   – frame 58

63 (67, 71)

Precision has been increased. Quite correct.

We have retrieved fewer non-relevant documents by being in the position to ignore documents dealing with other species of school.

We can say, therefore, that the *greater the specificity* achieved in indexing, *the higher will be the degree of precision* it is possible to achieve in response to a request.

Let us now suppose an increase in the exhaustivity of indexing, ie a move from the policy of summarization to one of depth indexing.

We shall now index documents under the term 'primary school' even if this concept is only embodied in a sub-theme within them.

In response to the request for information on the subject of primary schools we are now in a position to retrieve more documents than when following the policy of summarization. More documents will have been indexed under this concept.

What has been the effect of this increase in exhaustivity on recall?

Recall has been lowered   — frame 69
Recall has been increased   — frame 74

---

64 (49, 60, 62, 77)

You are correct. For example, wheat is just *one* kind of species of the genus cereals. Other species of this genus would be rye, barley, oats, etc. If we substitute the term cereal for wheat we would be losing specificity. Similarly, if we substitute 'mass media' for 'television' or 'transport' instead of 'land transport' specificity is lost.

It might be useful here to review briefly what we have said so far about subject analysis.

SUMMARY

SUBJECT ANALYSIS—also called conceptual analysis. The first stage in the indexing of a document. The recognition of concepts expressed in a document for the purposes of indexing the document. It is concerned with two characteristics of indexing.

EXHAUSTIVITY—the number of concepts contained within the document which are recognized for indexing purposes. The degree of exhaustivity employed in indexing is a policy decision. It may vary from,

SUMMARIZATION—a statement, or summary, of the dominant, overall theme of the document, to varying degrees of

DEPTH INDEXING—the policy of extracting all the important concepts contained within the document for indexing purposes. These concepts will be embodied in sub-themes of varying importance.

SPECIFICITY—the generic level at which a concept is indexed.

Continue on the next frame

The two characteristics of indexing, exhaustivity and specificity, affect two important measures of the *efficiency* of an information retrieval system.

These two measures, *RECALL* and *PRECISION*, operate at the search stage, or output stage, of the system.

Let us illustrate these terms by a hypothetical situation.

If *all* the documents in a collection, which are relevant to a request for information on a particular subject, are retrieved in response to that request, we have achieved 100% *RECALL*. (This is rarely, if ever, achieved; in any case it is rarely that a user really wants *everything* on the subject of his request.)

Theoretically, the only way of ensuring that *every* relevant document in a collection is retrieved, is to search *every* document in that collection.

This would mean that a great number of non-relevant documents would have to be searched and retrieved in order to retrieve the few relevant ones.

In this situation we would say that *PRECISION* was very low, ie precision in locating the relevant documents.

These two important measures of the efficiency of a retrieval system are quantified as:

RECALL RATIO. The recall ratio is the number of relevant documents retrieved, in proportion to the total number of relevant documents in the collection.

PRECISION RATIO. The precision ratio (originally called the *relevance ratio*) is the number of relevant documents retrieved, in proportion to the total number of documents searched and retrieved.

For example, if there are 10 relevant documents in a collection and of these 7 are retrieved the *recall ratio* is $\frac{7}{10}$ or 70%.

If 35 documents are retrieved in response to a request and, in fact, only 7 of these are relevant, the *precision ratio* is $\frac{7}{35}$ or 20%.

Suppose you have a request for information and there are 20 relevant documents in the collection. Your search results in a *recall ratio* of 75%. How many documents have you retrieved?

    10   — frame 59
    15   — frame 73
    12   — frame 68

66 (73)

You think you would have retrieved *10 relevant documents*. No, you are wrong.

Now remember that precision ratio is the number of relevant documents retrieved, in proportion to the total number of documents searched and retrieved.

Let us recalculate the example.

We said that 20 documents were retrieved, but only some of these proved relevant. These relevant documents produced a precision ratio of 40%.

If, as you said, 10 documents proved relevant, the precision ratio would be $\frac{10}{20}$ or 50%, not 40%.

If 8 documents were in fact relevant, the precision ratio would be $\frac{8}{20}$ or 40%.

Your answer should therefore have been 8 relevant documents.

Please turn to frame 70 and continue with the course.

---

67 (71)

You think that precision has been lowered. You must reconsider your decision.

Think of precision in indexing as precision in 'pin-pointing' relevant documents.

If we have to retrieve *all* the documents indexed under the term 'school', when we only want those about primary schools many of the documents retrieved will not be relevant. Precision will be low.

If, however, we index documents about primary schools under the term primary school, we can immediately rule out a lot of irrelevant documents in our search.

The substitution of 'primary school' for the term 'school' is an increase in the *specificity* of indexing.

Which of the following statements is true?

An increase in specificity leads to a decrease in precision	– frame 57
An increase in specificity leads to an increase in precision	– frame 63

68 (65)

You say that a recall ratio of 75% means that you have retrieved 12 documents. No, you are wrong.

Remember that recall ratio is the number of relevant documents retrieved, in proportion to the total number of relevant documents actually contained in the collection.

Now, in our example, we said that 20 relevant documents were contained in the collection and the search resulted in a recall ratio of 75%.

You say that 12 documents are therefore retrieved. But the retrieval of 12 documents out of a total of 20 relevant ones means a recall ratio of $\frac{12}{20}$ or only 60% not 75%.

Please return to frame 65. Recalculate and select the right answer.

---

69 (63, 72)

You say that recall has been lowered. Consider the problem again.

Remember that the recall ratio is the number of relevant documents retrieved in proportion to the total number of relevant documents contained in the collection.

The more of these relevant documents we can retrieve, the higher is our recall.

Now, if we are in a position to retrieve not only those documents dealing with a specified subject as their dominant theme, but also those that treat it as a sub-theme, we are in a position to increase recall.

In order to achieve this state, we must follow a policy of depth indexing rather than summarization. We must be more exhaustive in our indexing.

Which of the following statements is true?

By increasing exhaustivity we decrease recall   — frame 72
By increasing exhaustivity we increase recall   — frame 74

70 (61, 66, 73)

You have retrieved 8 relevant documents. Correct.

If you retrieve 20 documents but only 8 are relevant to the request, the precision ratio is $\frac{8}{20}$ or 40%.

To repeat,

Recall ratio is the number of relevant documents retrieved, in proportion to the total number of relevant documents in the collection.

Precision ratio is the number of relevant documents retrieved, in proportion to the total number of documents searched and retrieved.

An important relationship between these two measures is that they tend to vary *inversely.*

As recall is increased, precision is lowered and vice versa.

Continue on the next frame

---

71 (57, 70, 88)

We shall now consider how specificity and exhaustivity in indexing affect recall and precision.

Take a library in which the indexing policy is one of summarization, but the indexing of concepts is non-specific.

Thus, in the indexing of documents dealing with individual *kinds of school*—infant, primary, comprehensive etc—the term *school* has been used in all cases.

If a request is placed for information on 'primary schools' *all* documents indexed under the term 'school' must be searched and retrieved in order to retrieve the relevant documents.

Precision will consequently be low.

Suppose we now increase the specificity of the indexing. The concept 'primary school' is now indexed under 'primary school'—the species, not the genus.

In response to the request for information on this subject, it is only necessary to search and retrieve those documents indexed under the term 'primary school'.

Documents dealing with other species of school—infant, comprehensive, grammar etc can be ignored.

What has been the effect of this increase in specificity on precision?

Precision has been lowered   − frame 67
Precision has been increased   − frame 63

---

72 (69)

No. You have repeated your mistake.

Please return to frame 69, read the text carefully and attempt the question again.

73 (65)

You have retrieved 15 documents. Correct.

If there is a total of 20 relevant documents in the collection out of which you retrieve 15, the recall ratio is $\frac{15}{20}$ or 75%.

Now suppose you conduct a search which retrieves 20 documents, but out of which only a certain number prove relevant to the request. Your search results in a *precision ratio* of 40%. How many *relevant* documents have you retrieved?

 10   — frame 66
  8   — frame 70
 12   — frame 61

---

74 (63, 69, 87)

Recall has been increased. Correct.

If we retrieve *more* documents from the collection on the subject of the request, we increase recall.

An *increase in the exhaustivity* of indexing leads to an *increase in recall*.

However, although we can now retrieve more documents containing information on 'primary schools' than when following a policy of summarization, many of these documents will contain the concept only as a sub-theme.

They will contain relatively little information on the subject and the likelihood is that many of them will not in fact be relevant to the request, or to the needs of the user.

Consequently *precision* will be *lower*.

The tendency is for an *increase in recall* to result in a *decrease in precision* and vice versa.

In our practical subject indexing we shall be concerned first of all with subject analysis which limits exhaustivity to summarization but aims to make that summarization as specific as possible.

We shall thus be initially concerned with making a *SPECIFIC SUMMARIZATION* of the subject content of documents.

Continue on the next frame

75 (74)
TEST

Before continuing with the course, please answer the following series of questions. These will help you to check your understanding of some of the points dealt with so far in this section on subject analysis.

Consider your answers carefully. If you give a wrong answer you may be asked to revise the appropriate part of the text before proceeding.

Question 1
Which of the following statements is correct?

At the stage of the subject analysis of a document the concepts recognized are expressed in the terms of a language used for index descriptions. — frame 81

At the stage of the subject analysis of a document the concepts recognized are expressed in any convenient terms. — frame 84

---

76 (84)
Your answer: Exhaustivity refers to the number of concepts recognized for indexing purposes.

Correct.

Question 3
Which of the following could *not* be considered a genus/species relationship?

Teaching and remedial teaching — frame 83
Houses and three-storeyed houses — frame 85
Garden and gardening — frame 78

---

77 (86)
Your answer: Recall and precision are two methods of indexing for an information retrieval system.

No, this is not true. Please revise frames 64 and 65, then return to page 86 and select the right answer.

78 (76)

Your answer: The relationship between garden and gardening is *not* a genus/species relationship.

Correct.

The genus/species relationship is the relationship between a thing and its kinds. Gardening is an activity or operation not a *kind* of garden.

Question 4

Which of the following illustrates an increase in specificity?

Using gothic architecture instead of architecture   — frame 86
Using architecture instead of gothic architecture   — frame 89

---

79 (84)

Your answer: Specificity refers to the number of concepts recognized for indexing purposes.

No. You need to do some revision. Please turn to frame 48 and read the paragraphs on exhaustivity in indexing again. Then go to frame 84 and select the right answer.

---

80 (82)

Your answer: As the specificity of indexing is increased, precision increases.

Correct.

Question 7

A relationship is observable between the two measurements recall and precision. What is this relationship?

Recall and precision tend to vary proportionately.   — frame 87
Recall and precision tend to vary inversely.   — frame 90

---

81 (75)

You say that in the subject analysis of a document the concepts are expressed in the terms of a language used for index descriptions.

No, this is incorrect. Please go back and revise frame 40, then return to frame 75 and select the right answer.

82 (86)
Your answer: The terms recall and precision refer to two measurements of the efficiency of an information retrieval system.

Correct. The two measurements are quantified as the *recall ratio* and the *precision ratio*.

Question 6
Which of the following statements is correct?

As the specificity of indexing is increased, precision increases.   — frame 80

As the specificity of indexing is increased, precision decreases.   — frame 88

---

83 (76)
No, you are wrong. The relationship between teaching and remedial teaching is a genus/species relationship.

Remedial teaching is one species of the genus teaching.

Please return to frame 76 and select another answer.

---

84 (75)
Your answer: At the stage of subject analysis of a document, the concepts recognized are expressed in any convenient terms.

Correct. Often it is most convenient to use the terms employed by the author of the document.

Question 2
The term that refers to the number of concepts recognized for indexing purposes is

Specificity   — frame 79

Exhaustivity   — frame 76

---

85 (76)
No, this is incorrect. The relationship between houses and three-storeyed houses is a genus/species relationship.

A three-storeyed house is one species of the genus house.

Please return to frame 76 and select another answer.

86 (78)
Your answer: Using gothic architecture instead of architecture is an example of increasing specificity.

Correct. Gothic architecture is a species of the genus architecture. We would use the more precise term to increase the specificity of indexing.

Question 5
The terms *recall* and *precision* refer to

two methods of indexing for an information retrieval system	— frame 77
two measurements of the efficiency of an information retrieval system	— frame 82

---

87 (80)
Your answer: Recall and precision tend to vary proportionately.

No, this is not true. Revise frame 74 and then return to frame 80 and select the right answer.

---

88 (82)
Your answer: As the specificity of indexing is increased precision decreases.

No, you should go back and revise frame 71, then return to frame 82 and select the right answer.

---

89 (78)
Your answer: Using architecture instead of gothic architecture illustrates an increase in specificity.

No, you need to revise. Please re-read frame 49, then return to frame 78 and select the right answer.

---

90 (80)
Your answer: Recall and precision tend to vary inversely.

Correct. As recall is increased, precision tends to decrease and vice versa.

We trust that, if revision was suggested, you took this advice and that the points are now clear in your mind.

If you went through the test without any need for revision, so much the better.

You are now ready to go on to Part 2 of this section on Subject Analysis.

SECTION 2: SUBJECT ANALYSIS/PART II

In the subject analysis of documents we deal with a number of different *kinds* of concept.

The summarization of the overall theme of a document will usually not only consist of a number of individual concepts, these concepts will also be different in kind.

For example, a fairly straightforward document such as '*A medical dictionary of diseases*' would be summarized as:

MEDICINE/DISEASE/DICTIONARY

These three concepts are each representative of a different kind of concept. They each play a different role in the subject analysis.

The recognition of the distinctions between kinds of concepts, and of the roles they play in a subject analysis, is of fundamental importance in subject indexing.

It is to these problems that we must now turn our attention.

Continue on the next frame.

The first kind of concept to be considered is the *DISCIPLINE*. A DISCIPLINE is an area, or branch, of knowledge.

Chemistry, Zoology, Law and Sociology, for example, are all disciplines. They are all areas of human knowledge.

In the subject analysis of a document we must decide to which areas of knowledge, to which discipline it belongs and forms part of.

Thus, in our example '*A medical dictionary of diseases*', we should decide that the document belonged to the discipline medicine. This would appear as the first concept in the resulting summarization:

MEDICINE/DISEASE/DICTIONARY

Note that the discipline concept medicine is distinct from the *thing being studied* by this discipline. In this instance the thing being studied is disease. We shall turn to this distinction very shortly.

We can recognize two kinds of discipline. *FUNDAMENTAL DISCI-PLINES* and *SUB-DISCIPLINES*.

The FUNDAMENTAL DISCIPLINES constitute the major, primary divisions of knowledge.

There is not necessarily one accepted view as to the precise nature and number of the fundamental disciplines and this is not the place to pursue a lengthy discussion of the question. There is, however, general agreement as to the existence of these basic, and relatively stable, areas of knowledge, distinctive in kind and few in number.

P H Hirst, Professor of Education, University of Cambridge, using the four criteria of concepts used, logical structure, methodology and means of testing findings, defines eight such primary divisions of knowledge. These are:

Mathematics	Moral Knowledge
Physical Science	Art
Human Science	Religion
History	Philosophy

Continue on the next frame

93 (92)

The fundamental disciplines can be thought of as distinctive *kinds* of knowledge and can, in turn, be distinguished from their *SUB-DISCIPLINES*.

We can think of SUB-DISCIPLINES as areas of specialization within knowledge. They represent the application of one or more of the fundamental disciplines to particular sets of things being studied.

Examples of the sub-disciplines within Physical Science are biology, zoology, botany, physics. Within Human Science we find such sub-disciplines as economics and sociology; within Art, painting and music.

The sub-disciplines are obviously much greater in number than the fundamental disciplines and are the discipline concepts most frequently occurring in the subject analysis of documents.

Which is the more accurate definition of a discipline?

    A thing studied   — frame 100
    An area of knowledge   — frame 97

---

94 (97)

No, you have failed to draw the correct distinction between a discipline and a phenomenon studied by a discipline.

Geography is a discipline.

We might define this particular area of knowledge called geography by saying that it describes and analyses the landscape. It is thus a very wide ranging discipline studying the many diverse phenomena that together form the landscape, both physical and human.

Rivers, erosion, towns and glaciers are all phenomena studied by geography. So also is transport.

Now try another example. In the document '*The law of divorce*' which is the phenomenon concept?

    Law   — frame 98
    Divorce — frame 101

95 (102)

No, this is not correct.

We are drawing the distinction between these concepts that tell us what a document *is* and those that tell us what a document is *about*.

A *SUBJECT CONCEPT* constitutes part of the subject specification of a document. It states what a document is *about*.

A concept of *FORM* tells us what a document *is*, rather than what it is about.

A concept of *PHYSICAL FORM* tells us what a document is as a *physical entity*, eg a tape recording, film or book.

Now consider again the document titled '*The marketing of gramophone records*'. In this document, does the concept 'gramophone records' play the role of

     A subject concept?   − frame 106
     A form concept?   − frame 99

---

96 (111)

You are correct. The document is *about* first-aid, therefore we would say that this is a *subject concept*.

The subject of first aid is *presented for* the tourist. Tourist is thus a *form concept* indicating form of *presentation for a particular group of readers*.

It is quite common for document titles to provide an indication of the level of presentation of their subject in the use of such terms as 'Introduction', 'Primer', 'Popular', 'Advanced'.

Level of presentation is closely associated with the idea of form of presentation for a particular group of readers. It is, however, of much more general significance and is not usually recognized in the subject analysis of documents.

Please turn to frame 104 and continue with the course.

97 (93, 100)

You say that a discipline is defined as an area of knowledge. You are right.

We must now draw the distinction between disciplines and the *PHENOMENA*, or things, studied by disciplines. This distinction is of prime importance in subject indexing.

In the summarization of the document '*The psychology of the adolescent*', there are two concepts present, PSYCHOLOGY/ADOLESCENT. Psychology is the discipline concept, adolescent is the *PHENOMENON* being studied by this discipline.

The same phenomenon can be studied by a number of different disciplines. For example 'adolescent' could be studied by the disciplines of say education, psychology, medicine, economics or sociology, etc.

The phenomena studied by disciplines may be either *concrete entities* such as adolescent, motor car, dog or diamond or *abstract ideas* such as love, beauty or hate.

In the summarization of the document '*A geography of transport*' is transport

　　　　A discipline concept?　　　 – frame 94
　　　　A phenomenon concept?　　 – frame 101

---

98 (94)

No, you have repeated your mistake.

This is an important distinction which you must clarify before proceeding any further with the course.

Please turn to frame 97, read the text carefully and try the questions once more.

---

99 (95)

You say that the concept 'gramophone record' is, in this case, a form concept. No, you are wrong.

You have made the same mistake again.

Please return to frame 102 and read the explanations of form and subject concepts. Then try the questions once more.

100 (93)

You might refer to a discipline as a 'thing studied', but this is not the most *accurate* definition in our terms.

Atoms, mountains and men are also 'things studied', but they are not disciplines.

We reserve the term discipline to mean an area, or, if you like, a branch of knowledge.

Disciplines traditionally form the curricula for schools and universities, physics, history, sociology, law and so forth. As such you might say they are 'things' studied.

In indexing, however, 'things studied' means things studied *by disciplines*. Thus atoms, mountains and men are things studied by such disciplines as physics, geology or biology.

Remember, a discipline is an area of knowledge.

Now please turn to frame 97 where you will pursue this distinction between disciplines and the things studied by disciplines.

---

101 (94, 97)

You are correct.

Transport is a phenomenon studied, in this instance, by the discipline of geography, just as divorce is studied by law.

The phenomena studied by disciplines play the role of *SUBJECT CONCEPTS* in the subject analysis of documents. A subject concept tells us what a document is about. As we shall see, not all concepts in subject analysis do in fact perform this function. *'A geography of transport'* is, however, *about* transport, *'The psychology of adolescents'* is about adolescents.

SUMMARY

1 In the subject analysis of documents we can recognize different kinds of concept.
2 Disciplines, or areas of knowledge, can be recognized.
3 These may be either fundamental disciplines or sub-disciplines.
4 The phenomena studied by disciplines can be recognized.
5 These may be either concrete entities or abstract ideas.
6 Phenomena studied play the role of subject concepts, ie they tell us what a document is about.

Continue on the next frame

102 (101)

A subject concept tells us what a document is about. It constitutes a part of the *subject specification* of the document.

In contrast, a *FORM* concept tells us what a document *is*.

There are different kinds of form concept. The most obvious are the concepts of *PHYSICAL FORM*.

PHYSICAL FORM simply states the physical nature of a document. It tells us whether a document *is* a book or a pamphlet, a gramophone record or a photograph.

Physical form exerts no influence on the subjects of documents. If a document is *about* say, horse-racing, the fact that it *is* a film or a book does not alter the fact that its subject content *is* horse-racing.

Consider the document *'The marketing of gramophone records'*. Does the concept gramophone records tell us what the document *is*?

Yes — frame 95
No — frame 106

---

103 (108)

Motorist is here a *form* concept. Correct. The subject of the document is map-reading, ie it is *about* map-reading. This subject is being presented *for* a specialized target population, motorists.

It is quite common for document titles to provide an indication of the *level* of presentation of their subject in the use of such terms as 'Introduction', 'Primer', 'Popular', 'Advanced'.

Level of presentation is closely associated with the idea of form of presentation for a particular group of users. It is, however, of much more general significance and is not usually recognized in the subject analysis of documents.

Continue on the next frame

---

104 (96, 103)

Nothing has been said so far of the relationship between the *disciplines* and the ideas of subject and form.

The fundamental disciplines, history, art, science, philosophy etc, are distinctive *kinds* of knowledge. As such they can be said to constitute concepts of *INTELLECTUAL FORM*. They tell us what a document *is* rather than what it is *about*.

Macauley's *'History of England'* is *about* England. It *is* history in the sense that it is written within the discipline of history.

Unlike physical form and form of presentation, intellectual form *does* directly influence the subjects of documents. It does constitute an important part of the subject specification of documents.

Again, the same terms can represent either concepts of intellectual form or subject concepts. For example in the document '*A history of art*', art is the subject concept, the phenomenon studied, history is the intellectual form.

In the subject analysis of '*The philosophy of science*', which of the following is true?

Philosophy is the subject concept, science is the intellectual form   — frame 118

Science is the subject concept, philosophy is the intellectual form   — frame 114

---

105 (11)

No. You are still confusing subject concepts and form concepts.

Please return to frame 107 and go through the explanation of forms of presentation again. Then attempt the questions once more.

---

106 (95, 102)

You say that, in this instance, the concept 'gramophone record' does not tell us what the document *is*. You are correct.

'*The marketing of gramophone records*' is about gramophone records, it is not necessarily itself a gramophone record. We have no information as to the physical form of this document. In this case the term gramophone record represents a subject concept in the analysis of the document.

The most important point to note here is that the same terms can either represent concepts of physical form or subject concepts.

All documents possess physical form but this does not mean it is always taken cognisance of in subject analysis. Its significance in subject analysis for retrieval purposes is principally administrative. For example, certain physical forms require special storage facilities and the concept of physical form would then be noted. For most cases, for example with books, it can be ignored.

Continue on the next frame

The next group of form concepts are the *FORMS OF PRESENTATION*.

FORMS OF PRESENTATION are concepts which refer to the *organization* of the subject content of a document *within* any particular physical form.

We can recognize different *kinds* of forms of presentation.

Forms of symbol used for presentation:

These are

1 Language, eg English, Italian, Arabic
2 Mathematical, eg statistics, graphs, formulae
3 Pictorial, eg diagrams, drawings

Forms of arrangement, display or selection:

These are numerous and could be grouped as follows:

1 Order, eg alphabetical, chronological
2 'Literary' form, eg essays, lectures, letters
3 Reductions, eg abstracts, excerpts, synopsis
4 Collections, eg anthologies, encyclopaedias
5 'Keys', eg bibliographies, concordance, indexes
6 Rules, eg codes, specifications, standards

Again, care must be taken to distinguish whether a term represents the form of presentation of a document or the subject of a document.

In the case of '*An encyclopaedia of antiques*', 'antiques' is a subject concept, 'encyclopaedia' is a form concept. The document is *about* antiques, *presented in the form* of an encyclopaedia.

In '*The technique of writing abstracts*', 'abstracts' indicates the subject of the document, not its form of presentation.

The final kind of form of presentation, *PRESENTATIONS FOR PARTICULAR READERS*, is liable to cause the most confusion between subject and form.

Continue on the next frame

Such documents as '*Statistics for the geographer*' or '*Psychology for teachers*' are not *about* geography or teaching. They are about statistics and psychology.

The phrases 'for the geographer' and 'for the teacher' only serve to indicate that the subject of the documents are directed towards, or presented for, a particular group of readers, a specialized target population.

Look at the following document

'*The motorist's guide to map-reading*'

Is the concept motorist here

A subject concept?   — frame 111
A form concept?   — frame 103

109 (118)

You are quite right.

'*A history of religion*' is *about* religion and *is* history. That is it is written within the discipline of history.

History is therefore the *intellectual form* of this document.

Now please turn to frame 114 and continue with the course.

---

110 (113)

You say that the three phenomena, films, periodicals and gramophone records are *not* drawn from the same facet of librarianship. You are wrong.

A facet is defined by a single characteristic of division. These three phenomena are all materials held in the library. They therefore share this characteristic in common and all belong to the materials facet of librarianship.

Please return to frame 112 and read through the paragraphs on facets again. Then select another answer and proceed with the course.

---

111 (108)

You think that 'motorist' is a subject concept. No, this is not so.

The concept 'motorist' does not tell us what the document is *about*. The document is about map-reading. This subject, map-reading, is *presented for* the motorist, a particular group of readers.

Thus, 'motorist' is a form concept. It is a concept of *form of presentation* indicating the specialist group of readers towards whom the subject of the document is directed, or *presented for*.

Consider the following document, '*Essential first-aid for the tourist*'. Do you think that 'first-aid' is here a subject concept?

No   — frame 105
Yes   — frame 96

---

112 (117)

A category is a grouping of phenomena applicable to the whole, or a large part, of knowledge. Yes, this is the most precise definition of a category and the one we employ in this course.

When phenomena are considered in the context of a particular discipline, brought into a particular *context of study*, they can be grouped into more closely defined and named groups called *FACETS*. This is a very important term in subject indexing.

To illustrate a facet of a discipline let us take the subject area of medicine. Within this subject area we find, amongst others, such phenomena as heart, lungs, liver and brain. At the generalized level of categories, these phenomena can be regarded as manifestations of the category Entity. In the particular context of medicine, they constitute part of a *facet* of medicine which we can call *Part of body facet.*

Heart, lungs, liver and brain share a *characteristic in common*, they are all parts of the body.

Thus a FACET of a subject field consists of a number of phenomena within that subject which share some characteristic in common.

If we take the phenomena studied by a particular discipline and divide them into groups, or classes, on the basis of shared characteristics, the resulting groups or classes constitute the FACETS of that discipline.

The characteristic employed in the definition of a facet is consequently called a CHARACTERISTIC OF DIVISION and the resulting facet is named by its characteristic of division.

In our example from medicine we used the characteristic of division, 'Parts of the body', to define and name the 'Part of the body' facet. All the phenomena within this facet, —heart, liver, lungs, brain, kidneys etc— share this characteristic in common.

Continue on the next frame

---

113   (112)

We can, of course, recognize other facets within medicine. For example, influenza, measles, pneumonia share the common characteristic of being diseases. They therefore constitute part of the 'Disease' facet of medicine.

It is important to note that only *ONE* characteristic of division is applied in the definition of any given facet.

Thus in medicine we could not have a facet which contained *both* Parts of body *and* Diseases. These *two* characteristics of division produce *two* facets—the Parts of the body facet contains only parts of the body, the Disease facet contains only diseases.

Consider the subject field of librarianship. Let us say we can distinguish 3 facets within librarianship which we will call:

1   Type of library facet, eg public library
2   Materials (held in the library) facet, eg maps
3   Activities (conducted in the library) facet, eg indexing

In addition to these three there are the facets of Space, eg England, and Time, eg 1965, which are common to all subject areas.

In which of the following groups of phenomena are the three constituent phenomena *NOT* drawn from the same facet of librarianship?

Management, cataloguing, stock checking   — frame 119
Films, periodicals, gramophone records   — frame 110
Tape recordings, books, document selection   — frame 121

Science is the subject concept, philosophy the intellectual form. Quite right.

It was said earlier that the sub-disciplines can be regarded as the application of fundamental disciplines to particular sets of phenomena studied. Viewed in this light, they can be said to indicate *both* intellectual form *and* subject concepts.

> eg Title '*A textbook of botany*'
>
> Summarization: Botany

In the above example 'Botany' tells us that the document *is* in the intellectual form (fundamental discipline) Science and is *about* the phenomena plants.

SUMMARY

1 A form concept tells us what a document *is*.

2 Physical form and form of presentation do not influence the subjects of documents.

3 Intellectual forms do influence the subjects of documents.

4 Care must be taken to distinguish between terms representing form concepts and the same terms representing subject concepts.

Continue on the next frame

We shall now return to the phenomena studied by disciplines and look at these in a little more detail.

It was said that such phenomena might be either abstract ideas or concrete entities. In fact, any phenomenon you can think of could be an object of study by some disciplines or, more probably, by several disciplines. Initially, however, we shall consider these phenomena as concepts in their own right, divorced from and unrelated to any particular discipline or context of study.

We are thus concerned with a virtually limitless number of concepts— building, book, reading, colour, sea, water, summer, England, 1066 AD—any concept you like. At present we are not interested in their relationships to subject fields of which they can form a part—architecture, education, painting, meteorology, history etc.

These multitudinous phenomena can be divided into broad groups called *CATEGORIES*.

The term CATEGORY has been at times used somewhat loosely in the literature of indexing and, for this reason, it can cause confusion. We shall use it to mean a grouping of phenomena defined by their intrinsic nature, not by the role they play in a particular subject field.

There have been several ideas put forward as to just how many such categories exist and different terms have been used by different authorities in the naming of categories.

The Indian librarian and classificationist S R Ranganathan suggests that there are five categories of phenomena. These he names *Personality, Matter, Energy, Space* and *Time.*

We shall have more to say regarding these five categories when we look at Ranganathan's Colon Classification. At present we must emphasize Ranganathan's suggestion that *all* phenomena in *all* subject areas will be manifestations of either Personality or Matter or Energy or Space or Time. In other words, these five categories are applicable to *all* areas of knowledge. To stress this general applicability Ranganathan calls them the five *Fundamental Categories.*

Continue on the next frame

116 (115)

The categories of Space and Time are easily understandable. They contain concepts denoting, quite literally, space and time respectively. Personality, Matter and Energy are not so obvious and at this stage it is probably more acceptable to use the terminology *Entity, Property* and *Activity*.
These three categories bear a close correlation to Ranganathan's Personality, Matter and Energy categories.

The important point to remember concerning categories is that they are applicable to the grouping, or classification, of phenomena in all areas of knowledge. It is thus postulated that any given phenomenon in any given subject field can be regarded as either an Entity or a Property or an Activity or Space or Time. They are a valuable framework for the analysis of subject fields and of the relationships between the phenomena so analysed.

Other sets of categories containing more than just five have been suggested.

For example, we could have a set of categories such as Whole thing–Kinds (of a thing)–Parts (of a thing)–Materials–Properties–Processes–Operations–Agents–Space–Time.

These more detailed sets do not conflict with the more general sets of categories. They only represent refinements in the definition of categories of phenomena which result in *more* named categories. Thus the category Entity, for example, could be further refined into such categories as Whole thing–Kinds of thing–Parts of thing. These more detailed sets are often more particularly appropriate to the fields of science and technology; the more general sets are more generally applicable to the whole of knowledge.

Continue on the next frame

---

117 (116)

Which of the following statements defines the intrinsic nature of a category?

A category is a grouping of phenomena applicable
to only one area of knowledge   – frame 125
A category is a grouping of phenomena applicable
to the whole, or a large part, of knowledge   – frame 112

118 (104)

You think that philosophy is the subject concept and science the intellectual form. This is not true.

Philosophy and science are both fundamental disciplines, they are both distinctive *kinds* of knowledge.

We are concerned here in distinguishing the fundamental disciplines in their roles as *intellectual forms* in the subject analysis of documents.

We can regard a fundamental discipline as an intellectual form when it tells us *what kind of knowledge* the document *is*, rather than what it is *about*.

Science or philosophy or art, etc, are intellectual forms when they indicate that the document *is* science or philosophy or art and not *about* these disciplines.

Consider the document titled '*A history of religion*'. This document is about religion. History is the

Subject concept	– frame 126
The concept of intellectual form	– frame 109

---

119 (113)

You say that the three phenomena, management, cataloguing and stock checking are *not* drawn from the same facet of librarianship. You are wrong.

A facet is defined by a single characteristic of division. These three phenomena are all *activities* carried out in the library. They therefore share this characteristic in common and all belong to the *activities facet* of librarianship.

Please return to frame 112 and read through the paragraphs on facets again. Then select another answer and proceed with the course.

---

120 (124)

You say that the document '*Secondary education*' is an example of a compound subject. You are wrong.

A compound subject consists of a basic subject plus isolates from MORE THAN ONE facet of that subject.

Had the document been about '*The use of audio-visual aids in secondary education*', we would have a summarization such as:

Education/Secondary/Audio-visual aids

This is an example of a compound subject. 'Education' constitutes the basic subject; 'Secondary' and 'Audio-visual aids' are isolates drawn from facets of this area of knowledge.

The document in question was titled '*Secondary education*', giving the summarization:

Education/Secondary

Here we only have ONE isolate, secondary, drawn from one facet of the basic subject Education.

Thus we have an example of a SIMPLE subject.

Now please turn to frame 127 and continue with the course.

---

121 (113)

You say that the phenomena tape recordings, books and book selection are not drawn from the same facet of librarianship. You are quite correct.

Books and tape-recordings are both types of materials held in libraries. They share this characteristic in common and belong to the Materials facet, defined by this characteristic of division.

Document selection, however, is an activity conducted in the library and therefore belongs to what we called the Activities facet.

We can here introduce a convenient term applied by Ranganathan to the elementary concepts which together make up the facets of a subject area— ISOLATES.

Books, indexing, heart, disease etc, are all ISOLATES, that is they are capable of being considered in isolation, unrelated to any particular subject area.

When brought into the context of a given subject area they form isolates within the facets of that subject.

eg heart forms an *isolate* within the *Part of body facet* of the *subject area* medicine.

By virtue of sharing the same characteristics of division, the isolates within a facet all stand in the same *relation* to their subject area or *containing class.*

For example, they are all entities within that subject area, or all activities etc.

Thus, in recognizing the existence of categories and facets we, at the same time, recognize that elementary concepts stand in various relationships to one another.

Continue on the next frame

---

122 (121)

These relationships are broadly divisible into two types.

First there is the *genus/species relationship* which we have already met.

This is the relationship which exists between the isolates within the *same* facet and the type of concept which defines the facet, the concept employed as its characteristic of division.

For example, all the isolates in the Disease facet of medicine, tuberculosis, stroke etc, are all *species* or *kinds* of *disease.* All the isolates within the Libraries facet of library science are *species* or *kinds* of *library.* Thus the relationship between library and kinds of library or between disease and kinds of disease is the relationship of a genus to its species, of a thing to its kinds.

Second is the varied group of relationships which exist between isolates from *different* facets.

Examples of these kinds of relationships are those between a Thing and an Activity.

These relationships between concepts play an important role in subject indexing and we shall have continuing reference to them. At this stage we should note that they exist as an integral part of the subject analysis of documents.

Continue on the next frame

---

123 (122)

Before you go on to subject analyse some individual documents and produce specific summarization of their overall theme, there are one or two final points to be made concerning the nature of the 'subject of documents'.

The discipline, that is the area of knowledge to which a document belongs, gives the document its BASIC SUBJECT.

The summarized subject of a document may consist of its basic subject

    eg   Title: '*A textbook of physics*'
          Summarization: Physics

In this case the basic subject alone, physics, suffices to name the summarized subject of the document. No individual phenomena studied in this subject area, eg heat, light, sound, magnetism, electricity etc are named in the summarization. It implies that the document deals with the whole of that subject area and does not concentrate on any particular phenomenon or phenomena within it.

If the summarized subject of a document consists of its basic subject and ONE isolate drawn from ONE facet of that area of knowledge, it is called a SIMPLE SUBJECT.

    eg   Title: '*The physics of light*'
          Summarization: Physics/Light

The majority of subjects produced by the summarization of documents consists of a basic subject and isolates drawn from TWO OR MORE facets of that subject.

These are called COMPOUND SUBJECTS.

    eg   Title: '*The curriculum in primary schools*'
          Summarization: Education/Primary/Curriculum

This is an example of a compound subject in which education is the basic subject and the isolates 'primary' and 'curriculum' are drawn from two facets of this subject area.

Continue on the next frame

124 (123)
Now look at the following example:

Title: *'Secondary education'*
Summarization: Education/Secondary

Which type of subject is this an example of?

A simple subject   – frame 127
A compound subject   – frame 120

---

125 (117)
You think that a category is a grouping of phenomena applicable to only *one* area of knowledge. No, this is not the case.

This definition would imply that the category of phenomena called Entities is only found in one area of knowledge, say, for example, biology.

In this course we use the term category with a more basic and fundamental implication for the analysis of knowledge.

Because this term is used rather loosely in the literature of classification, and because it represents a very important idea, it is wise to clarify its definition at this stage.

Please return to frame 115 and read carefully through the explanation of categories. Then select the correct answer to the question and proceed with the course.

---

126 (118)
No, you are still not clear in your mind about the fundamental disciplines as concepts of intellectual form.

Please return to frame 104. Resume the course from this point and attempt the question again.

127 (120, 124)

Yes, the summarization of *'Secondary education'* presents an example of a simple subject.

It possesses one isolate, secondary, in addition to the basic subject education.

A compound subject consists of a *basic subject plus isolates from more than one facet of that subject.* A simple subject consists of a *basic subject plus an isolate from only one facet of that subject.*

Care must be taken not to confuse compound subjects with *COMPOSITE DOCUMENTS.*

COMPOSITE DOCUMENTS are documents which contain *two or more discrete subjects.*

For example, a document *'Mathematics and physics'* which deals with these two subject fields as two distinct disciplines is a composite document.

Thus *composite* refers to the nature of a *document, compound* refers to the nature of the *subject of a document.*

Continue on the next frame

---

128 (127)

You are now in a position to attempt the subject analysis of some documents for yourselves. In a real library situation you would, of course, have the documents themselves but this is impractical in a course of this nature.

Your analysis will consist of elementary concepts which, together, will produce a *summarization of the overall theme of a document.*

Remember that this summarization should be a *specific summarization.* The elementary concepts which you decide constitute a specific summarization of the document should be written down in the following order:

1 The concept denoting the area of knowledge or discipline to which the document belongs—this gives us the basic subject or basic class of the document.

2 Isolates denoting the phenomena studied by the basic subject, including isolates of Space and Time, which should appear last in this group.

3 Isolates denoting Form which should appear last of all in the string of concepts as they do not affect the subjects of the documents.

It is useful to employ some device, such as an oblique stroke (/), to separate clearly the elementary concepts in the summarization.

Continue on the next frame

Before you attempt your own analysis, here are three examples which help to illustrate the procedure once more.

Title: *'A book of Mediterranean food'*
Summarization: Domestic science/Food/Cookery/Mediterranean/ Recipes

In this example Domestic science gives us the basic subject of the document. Food, cookery and Mediterranean are isolates drawn from the facets of Domestic science, constituting phenomena studied. Recipes is an isolate denoting form, in this case it is the form of presentation of the subject.

Title: *'First and last loves'*
Summarization: Architecture/Gt Britain/Victorian/Essays

In the artificial situation of not having actual documents to hand to work with, it may be wise to remind ourselves that classification cannot usually be done by relying on the title alone. This title is hardly self-explanatory. The book is, in fact, a collection of essays by John Betjeman on Victorian architecture in Great Britain.

Title: *'Itself an education: six lectures on classification'*
Summarization: Library science/Classification/Lectures

This is the sort of title we have to rely on in this context. One that is largely self-explanatory and therefore makes the task of subject analysis easier by indicating the subject content.

Now try the following examples for yourself. Then turn over the page where you will find suggested analyses against which you can check your solutions.

1   Education in Scotland 1960
2   Inter-library cooperation in England and Wales
3   Library resources in the Greater London area, No 5: Agricultural libraries
4   The Radio Doctor's dictionary of health
5   A handbook of heart disease, blood pressure and strokes: the causes, treatment and prevention of these disorders

Subject analysis, in the form of specific summarization, of document titles given in frame 129.

1   Education/Scotland/1960
2   Library science/Library cooperation/England and Wales
3   Library science/Special libraries/Agriculture/Greater London
4   Medicine/Health/Dictionary
    You may have regarded this as simply a dictionary of medicine:

    Medicine/Dictionary

    This would be quite acceptable. More important is to note that the fact that it is the Radio Doctor's dictionary has no relevance for its subject content.
5   Medicine/Cardiovascular system/Diseases/Handbook
    This is the most difficult example. The above analysis is a *summarization*. If you have included such concepts as heart disease or treatment etc, you have gone beyond summarization into the levels of depth indexing.

Do not worry about the words you have used in your subject analyses. Remember that, at the stage of subject analysis you use whatever words you choose to name concepts. Nor need you be particularly concerned, as yet, about the order in which you have stated your concepts. This question of order will be dealt with in the next section of the course to which you should now proceed.

Continue on the next frame

SECTION 3: THE ELEMENTS OF PRACTICAL CLASSIFICATION

In this section of the course you will be concerned with the second stage in the practical subject indexing of documents. This is the stage of the *translation* of the subject analysis of a document into the terms of a particular *indexing language.*

There are different kinds of indexing language. The kind that we are concerned with here is the classification scheme. The techniques that you will learn in this section of the course are therefore the techniques of *practical classification.*

The Colon Classification is the scheme that will be used to introduce the techniques of practical classification and to demonstrate some of the principles of classification.

There will be more to say later about the reasons for the choice of this scheme. However, it should be stated at the outset that it is *not* the aim of this course to make you proficient in the use of the Colon Classification as a practical indexing language. The scheme is used only as a suitable vehicle for the demonstration of principles and techniques. You do not require to possess a copy of this scheme in order to follow the course.
Continue on the next frame

At the first stage of indexing a document, subject analysis, the indexer expresses concepts in whatever words, or terms, he chooses. Very often it is most convenient to use the terms employed by the author of the document.

There are thus *no controls* placed upon the indexer in his choice of terms. He can use 'medicine' *or* 'medical science', 'wireless' *or* 'radio' to express the desired concepts.

Having completed his subject analysis, as in, for example, a summarization of the document's overall theme, the indexer proceeds to the second stage of practical subject indexing, namely, *TRANSLATION.*

Translation is the process of converting the terms used by the indexer in his subject analysis of a document into the words, or code numbers, of a *controlled language.* That is, translation into an *INDEXING LANGUAGE.* The translated subject analysis, either in the form of words or of code numbers, will constitute the index description of the document. These index descriptions of documents will be used, for example, for the arrangement of documents on the shelves and for the arrangement of catalogue entries.

By utilizing the same indexing language, the *searcher* is able to define the concepts being looked for in the same words or code numbers as were used by the *indexer* in his index descriptions of documents.

Why do you think that concepts must be translated in subject indexing?

So that the indexer will define the author's
concepts precisely   — frame 135

So that the indexer and searcher can
represent concepts in the same way   — frame 136

So that the searcher's needs will be
specified precisely   — frame 139

---

133   (138, 143)

You say that notation *reflects* the classified order of terms. This is right. The classified order of terms is a schedule not *determined* by the notation. The notation is a convenient method of maintaining and reflecting this order.

In order to locate any given concept within the schedules, a classification scheme must be provided with an *alphabetical index.* This is an alphabetical arrangement of concepts which gives their respective notations and thus their exact position within the schedules.

We have reproduced a sample page from the CC index on frame 200 of this book. If you consult this page of the index under the word 'trigonometry' you will see that this concept has the notation B5. This tells us that this concept can be located in the schedules under Chapter B, Mathematics, at the precise notation B5.

Do not worry that many of the notations given alongside terms in the index appear complex and may be difficult to locate. The meanings of these notational instructions will become apparent as you progress.

As this stage you need only appreciate that the index, by listing terms in an alphabetical order, serves as a key to the classified order of concepts in the schedules.

CC is a *general* classification scheme. A general classification scheme provides for the whole universe of knowledge, it deals with all subject areas. Classification schemes which deal only with restricted areas of knowledge, such as education, management or library science, are called *special classifications.*

As a general scheme, CC is potentially capable of classifying the subjects of documents belonging to any area of knowledge.

Continue on the next frame

134 (133, 154)

You have seen in your study of subject analysis, that the majority of subjects expressed in documents are *compound*, that is they consist of a basic subject and one or more of its isolates.

Now look again at that part of the CC schedules devoted to the subject area of library science, on frame 199.

You will see that CC lists, and provides notations for only the isolate concepts present in this subject area. If you look down the two columns you will see only isolate concepts, eg classification, cataloguing, book selection, etc.

CC does not list, or *enumerate*, compound subjects as found in documents, eg

> '*Book selection in university libraries*'
> '*Cataloguing of periodicals*'

In order to classify a compound subject by CC, the indexer must first *analyse* the subject into its elementary constituents. He must then locate these individual elements in the CC schedules and recombine, or *synthesize*, them to form the compound subject expressed in notational terms.

Classification schemes which are based upon the principles of analysis and synthesis are called *ANALYTICO-SYNTHETIC* (or faceted) classifications.

Many classification schemes do list, or enumerate, compound subjects. They attempt to provide ready-made notations for compound subjects as found expressed in documents.

Classification schemes which are enumerative of compound subjects are commonly called *ENUMERATIVE* classifications.

Which of the following statements is true?

CC is an analytico-synthetic classification	– frame 145
CC is an enumerative classification	– frame 151

---

135 (132)

You think that concepts must be translated so that the indexer will define the author's concepts precisely.

It is true that the indexer must be precise in his definition of the concepts treated by the author of the document. An indexing language may well help the indexer to clarify his definitions of the author's concepts but this is not its main purpose, nor is it necessary to translate into such a language in order to achieve precision in such definitions.

The searcher for information cannot, however, be expected to know what words the indexer has used in his initial subject analysis of a document. An indexing language provides a standard that both indexer and searcher can use.

Please return to frame 132 and read about translation into indexing languages again. Then reconsider the question and select another answer.

136 (132)
You are correct. The translation of concepts into the words or code numbers of an indexing language enables the indexer and the searcher to express those concepts in the same manner.

This is a necessary condition for the effective retrieval of information.

The index description of a document is expressed in words or code numbers determined by an indexing language. If the concepts being searched for are expressed in the same way, an effective match can be achieved between the index description and the search prescription.

As indexing languages are used both in the indexing of documents and in the search programming which leads to their subsequent retrieval they are sometimes referred to as *retrieval languages.*

In this course we shall use the term indexing language.

Continue on the next frame

---

137 (136)
There are two major aspects of every indexing language. These are:
1 the *vocabulary*—the terms selected for the indexing of concepts
2 the *syntax*—the methods employed to indicate the relationships between the concepts indexed.

You will become increasingly familiar with these aspects as you gain experience in the use of indexing languages.

Although indexing languages take a variety of forms, common to all and the basis of all, is the *controlled vocabulary* of indexing terms.

In certain kinds of indexing language these terms are arranged in alphabetical order. The exact location of any term in such languages is determined by its position in the alphabetical sequence of terms, as in a dictionary.

The terms may, however, be arranged, or grouped, according to the *ideas* they express as in, for example, Roget's thesaurus. In this case they are arranged in a *classified order.*

The first kind of indexing language you will use is the *classification scheme* and this employs a classified order to terms.

We shall now look at the Colon Classification as our first example of a classification scheme.

Continue on frame 140

138 (143)

You say that notation *provides* a classified order for terms. This is not the case.

The schedules of a classification scheme consist of terms grouped according to the concepts or ideas they represent. Thus, at a simple level, terms representing mathematical concepts, might be arranged together in a class consisting of the discipline mathematics.

There are many possible ways of arranging terms in a classified order. An individual classification scheme, like Colon, represents one chosen and preferred order.

Once the particular classified order of terms has been decided upon, only at this stage in the making of a classification scheme, is the *notation* added.

Remember, therefore, that notation does not *provide* the classified order. This order stems from the nature of the concepts themselves.

The notation of a classification scheme is only a means of maintaining this classified order and of identifying the position of any term within it. Please turn to frame 133 and continue with the course.

---

139 (132)

You think that concepts must be translated so that the searcher's needs will be specified precisely.

Reference to an indexing language may help the searcher refine his definition of concepts, but this is by no means the main purpose of translation into an indexing language.

In order to locate relevant information, however, the searcher must know how concepts have been expressed in the index description of documents. The use of an indexing language provides a means of expressing concepts that both indexer and searcher can refer to.

You should now return to frame 132 and read again about translation into indexing languages. Then reconsider the question and select another answer.

COLON CLASSIFICATION

The Colon Classification was devised by the eminent Indian librarian and classificationist the late S R Ranganathan. The first edition of the scheme was published in 1933 and later modified through several editions. The edition that you will be referred to in this course is the 6th, first published in 1960.

The work of Ranganathan has been the most important single factor influencing modern library classification. Much of the terminology used in this course, for example, was first introduced by Ranganathan. Its usage has now become standard practice.

Many of Ranganathan's ideas which have had this wide and fundamental influence on the theory and practice of classification are embodied in his Colon Classification. It is for this reason that you are being introduced to practical classification through the medium of this scheme.

It is *not* the aim of this course to make you an expert in the use of the Colon Classification. It is intended that you should be acquainted with the basic structure of the scheme and the most important principles which underlie it. The ability you will attain to translate into Colon will reflect this basic understanding only.

Your practice in classifying by Colon will, however, have a direct bearing on any subsequent use of other classification schemes. It will help you to use those schemes with greater understanding and, therefore, more effectively.

From this point on in the text the Colon Classification will be referred to by the commonly used abbreviation CC.

Continue on the next frame

Unfortunately, copies of the 6th edition of CC are now difficult to purchase. It is *not* therefore assumed that you have access to a copy of the scheme. In order that you may follow this programmed text without possessing a copy of CC, extracts from the scheme have been included in this book on frames 196-200. From now on you will be referred to these extracts and so it would be helpful for you to place a bookmark by frame 196.

In order to set our extracts in their true context, and for the benefit of those readers who *do* have access to the scheme, there follows a brief description of the physical structure of the 6th edition. The 6th edition was reprinted with amendments in 1963 and it is this amended version which will be described and referred to. References to page numbers in CC itself will be made in parentheses.

The reprinted 6th edition contains a general Introduction (CC pages 12-16) and then an Annexure (CC pages 19-28). The Annexure contains some changes and corrections to the 6th edition as it first appeared in 1960.

CC is then divided into three numbered Parts:

Part 1/Rules
This section (found by turning to CC page 28) contains explanations of the scheme and instructions as to its use. Each main class of the scheme has an individual chapter devoted to it in Part 1 (between pages 1.62 and 1.222). These chapters tell you how the class is constructed and how it is to be used, often with exemplification. There is an index to this first part of the scheme (CC page 1.123).

Although essential to the full use of CC, much of Part 1 goes into a degree of detail which is beyond the requirements of this course.

Continue on the next frame

---

142 (141)
Part 2/Schedules of classification
This section (immediately following CC page 1.124) constitutes the main body of the classification scheme and is therefore the part with which you will be most concerned. It contains the schedules of classification and their necessary alphabetical indexes. We shall return to this part in more detail very shortly.

Part 3/Schedules of classics and sacred books with special names
This part (following CC page 2.172) provides detailed schedules mainly for use in the classification of Indian classics and sacred books. It contains its own alphabetical index (beginning on CC page 3.54)

Due to its highly specialized nature, this section of the scheme has no direct relevance to your particular needs in this course.

If you possess a copy of CC it would be advisable for you to look through it at this stage and acquaint yourself with the general appearance of each Part before proceeding further.

The way in which this scheme is put together in book form often causes some confusion at first. Practice in its use soon leads to familiarity with the various parts of the book, however.

Note the method of page numbering employed. Each page number contains a Part number and then the number of the individual page within that Part following a decimal point. Thus page 1.88 is page 88 of Part 1, page 2.103 is page 103 of Part 2, etc.

Continue on the next frame

143 (142)

We shall now look more closely at Part 2 of the scheme, the Schedules of Classification. The list of terms, representing concepts which will be indexed, constitutes the *SCHEDULES* of a classification scheme.

The terms in the schedules are arranged in classified order. That is they are grouped according to the concepts, or ideas, which they represent.

A classification scheme assigns *code numbers* to the terms in its schedules. These code numbers identify the positions of terms within the classified arrangement.

Now turn to frame 199 where you will see reprinted the schedule for the subject area Library science (CC page 2.30). You need not worry about the way in which the terms in this schedule are grouped for the present. A cursory glance at the first column on this page of the schedules shows you that the terms listed here have a code number assigned to each, eg 1 is Trans-local, 11 is World, 13 Nation, etc. Such code numbers make up the *NOTATION* of a classification scheme. The notation of a classification scheme does not determine the order of terms in its schedules. The classified order is decided upon first.

The notation provides a convenient method of maintaining this arrangement of terms and of identifying their positions within the classified order. The schedules of a classification scheme thus consist of a classified arrangement of terms, each being identified by their respective code number or notation.

Which of the following best describes the function of a notation?

It provides a classified order for terms   — frame 138
It reflects the classified order of terms   — frame 133

---

144 (153)

You say that 'university' is a focus in the Matter facet of class 2 Library science.

Foci in the Matter facet of a class are listed under the instruction *'Foci in (M)'*. You will not find the concept 'university' listed under this instruction within the schedule for Library science. It therefore does not belong to the Matter facet of this class.

Please return to frame 153. Read the question once more, check the schedule carefully and select another answer.

You are right. CC is an analytico-synthetic classification scheme.

CC does *not* enumerate compound subjects and provide them with ready-made notations.

When dealing with such subjects, practical classification with CC involves more than simply looking up the subject in the index, checking its position in the schedules and writing down the notation.

It is the task of the indexer first to analyse the subject into its elementary constituents and then to synthesize these from the schedules into a notational expression of the compound.

You have already examined the procedures of subject analysis, unrelated to any particular indexing language.

We must now look at the ways in which CC analyses subjects in its schedules. This is the first step in learning to use the scheme for the purposes of practical subject indexing.

Continue on the next frame

CC first of all divides the whole of knowledge into disciplines, traditionally recognized fields of study.

These primary divisions constitute the *MAIN CLASSES* of the scheme.

The following is a list of the main classes of CC with their respective notations (this list is to be found on CC page 2.4).

z	Generalia	LX	Pharmacognosy
1	Universe of knowledge	M	Useful arts
2	Library science	Δ	Spiritual experience and
3	Book science		mysticism
4	Journalism	MZ	Humanities and social
A	Natural sciences		sciences
AZ	Mathematical sciences	MZA	Humanities
B	Mathematics	N	Fine arts
BZ	Physical sciences	NX	Literature and languages
C	Physics	O	Literature
D	Engineering	P	Linguistics
E	Chemistry	Q	Religion
F	Technology	R	Philosophy
G	Biology	S	Psychology
H	Geology	Σ	Social science
HX	Mining	T	Education
I	Botany	U	Geography
J	Agriculture	V	History
K	Zoology	W	Political science
KX	Animal husbandry	X	Economics
L	Medicine	Y	Sociology
		YX	Social work
		Z	Law

These main classes include both fundamental disciplines, eg V History, and sub-disciplines, eg I Botany.

Not all the main classes listed are developed in the schedules of the 6th edition. This need not concern us.

Continue on the next frame

147   (146)
Some of these main classes are further divided into traditionally recognized sub-fields within the area of study which constitutes the main class.

Such subdivisions of a main class are called *CANONICAL DIVISIONS*. For example, class R Philosophy (CC page 2.100) is first divided into such canonical divisions as R1 Logic, R2 Epistemology, R3 Metaphysics, R4 Ethics and R5 Aesthetics.

Continue on the next frame

---

148   (147)
Within some main classes CC recognizes that the *entire* subject field can be studied from different philosophical and theoretical viewpoints or '*systems of thought*'. These divisions of a main class are called *SYSTEMS FACETS*.

For example, class T Education is provided with such systems facets as TL5 the Pestalozzi School and TN1 the Montessori School. (These can be found on CC page 2.106 under 'TA Systems').

CC also recognizes that certain areas of study which constitute main classes often specialize in only a part of their potential coverage. Provisions for this kind of main class division are called *SPECIALS FACETS*.

For example, class L Medicine has such specials facets as L9C Child medicine and L9F Female medicine. (These can be found on CC page 2.86 under 'L9A Specials').

Continue on the next frame

---

149   (148)
All the divisions of knowledge so far mentioned—the main classes themselves, canonical divisions, systems and specials facets—are based upon the principle of dividing knowledge into subject fields or areas of study.

We now come to the ways in which CC analyses and arranges the *phenomena* studied by the subject fields which constitute its main classes.

The phenomena studied by subject fields are listed as isolate concepts within the main class schedule for that subject.

Within each main class, the isolates are grouped into *facets* of the subject field.

You have already met the term facet. Which was the definition that we applied to this term?

A facet is a group of isolates which share some
characteristic in common.   — frame 152
A facet is a group of isolates which together
form a compound subject.   — frame 156

So far we have only attempted to locate elementary concepts in the CC schedules. This helps to illustrate the methods of analysis employed by the scheme and to introduce the mechanics of its use.

We shall now begin to examine the ways in which we can express the *compound subjects* of documents by CC notation. The notational expression of a subject is called its *CLASS NUMBER* or *CLASS MARK.*

In CC each facet is introduced, notationally, by its own *FACET INDICATOR.* In the notation of this scheme punctuation marks are used as facet indicators and these serve to individualize the respective facets.

    Personality has the facet indicator , (comma)
    Matter has the facet indicator   ; (semi-colon)
    Energy has the facet indicator   : (colon)

Let us take a simple example to illustrate the use of facet indicators in CC:

    Document title: *'Teaching techniques'*
    Subject analysis (summarization):   Education/Teaching techniques
    Class number: T : 3

In the above compound subject 'teaching technique' is an isolate in the Energy facet of class T Education.

In the class number we must use the facet indicator for Energy to introduce the isolate number from this facet of class T.

Now look at the following example:

    Title   *'Classification in librarianship'*
    Subject analysis   Library science/Classification

Which of the following is the correct CC class number for the compound subject of this document?

    2 ; 51   – frame 169
    2   51   – frame 157
    2 : 51   – frame 164

No, this is not so. CC is not referred to as an enumerative classification.

We said that an enumerative classification scheme is characterized by its enumeration, or listing, of compound subjects. That is, it attempts to provide a ready-made location in its schedules, complete with a notation, for such subjects as *'Book selection in university libraries'* or *'Cataloguing of periodicals'.*

Now if you look again at CC, page 2.30, the schedules for Library science, you will see that only isolate concepts are listed and provided with notations, eg Book selection, University, Cataloguing.

Which of the following statements is therefore true?

    CC enumerates compound subjects   – frame 154
    CC does not enumerate compound subjects   – frame 145

A facet is a group of isolates which share some characteristics in common. Correct.

A facet of a subject field is defined by the application of a *characteristic of division*. All the isolates in the resulting facet share this characteristic in common. For example, they are all diseases, or all kinds of library or all crops etc.

Because CC analyses subjects according to the principles of facet analysis, it is called a *FACETED* classification scheme.

You will remember Ranganathan postulates that all isolates in all areas of knowledge belong to one of five Fundamental Categories—Personality, Matter, Energy, Space or Time. These are commonly referred to by their initial letters P M E S T.

In the CC schedules the facets of a subject area are *named* according to whether their constituent isolates are manifestations of P M E S or T. We thus have the *Personality facet* of a subject, the *Energy facet* and so on.

The concept of Fundamental Categories plays a very important role in practical subject indexing. Initially you will probably have some difficulty in deciding just which category a particular isolate belongs to in a particular subject context. As you gain experience in practical classification this difficulty will recede.

Space and *Time* isolates are usually quite explicit and easy to distinguish. We shall not pursue them further just yet.

Energy (E) isolates include such concepts as operations, activities, problems and processes.

Matter (M) isolates are the least common. They denote the physical materials and properties in a subject field.

Personality (P) isolates are perhaps the most difficult of all to recognize and yet, in certain respects, they are the most important. Personality isolates are those which characterize a subject area and give it its individuality.

These brief, generalized statements will become more meaningful as you examine actual manifestations of PMES and T in the CC schedules and in the subject analysis of documents.

Categories in general, and Ranganathan's five Fundamental Categories in particular, were first mentioned on frame 115 of Section 2 of this book. It might be wise for you to turn back and re-read what was said there. We said that the terms 'Personality', 'Matter' and 'Energy' corresponded closely to the terms Entity (or Thing), Property and Activity. Terms used by the Classification Research Group to name categories.

As the concept of Personality is particularly difficult to envisage, at least on initial acquaintance, it may be helpful for you to think of it as representing Entities or Things.

In a similar way Matter relates broadly to the category of Properties and Energy to the category of Activities.

Continue on the next frame

153 (152)

In the schedules of each main class, CC groups the isolates into the P M and E facets of that class. Each isolate within a facet is called a *FOCUS* of that facet.

The instruction '*Foci in P*' tells you that the isolates listed here are *foci* in the *Personality facet*.

'*Foci in M*' indicates a *Matter facet*.

An *Energy facet* is usually indicated by the instruction '*Foci in E cum 2P*'. You can ignore the 'cum 2P' part of this instruction at present.

For example, in class T Education (CC page 2.105) the instruction '*Foci in P*' is followed by a list of isolates including such as *pre-school child, adult, abnormal* etc. These are all types of person receiving education, or educand, and they constitute the Personality facet of class T Education.

Turn now to the schedule for class 2 Library science on frame 199 (CC pages 2.30) and locate in the schedule the isolate 'university'.

Of which facet of Library science is university a focus?

Energy facet	– frame 163
Matter facet	– frame 144
Personality facet	– frame 159

---

154 (151)

No. You are still confused about compound subjects and their enumeration in the schedules of classification schemes.

Please return to frame 134, read through the text again and attempt the questions once more.

---

155 (168)

You say that 233;17:55 is the correct class number. You are wrong.

The correct use of facet indicators is observed in this class number but you have not checked the schedules carefully enough to obtain the right *isolate number* for the concept 'university libraries'.

Look at the schedule for class 2 again and you will see that *your* class number represents the subject of the document,

'*Map cataloguing in college libraries*'

The correct class number should have been

234;17:55

It is extremely important to check the schedules carefully and to work accurately with notation.

Please turn to frame 166 and continue with the course.

156 (149)

You say that we defined a facet as a group of isolates which together form a compound subject.

No, this is wide of the mark.

A facet is a group of isolates which share some characteristics in common.

The concept of a facet is an extremely important one in classification. You are advised to return to Section 2 Part II, Subject Analysis, and revise the explanation of facets which you will find on frame 112.

You may proceed with your examination of CC by turning to frame 152.

---

157 (150)

Your answer 251. No, this is wrong.

You have failed to observe the correct use of facet indicators in the construction of your class number.

Classification occurs as a concept in the *Energy* facet of class 2, Library science. It must therefore be introduced by the facet indicator reserved for Energy.

Please return to frame 150. Read through the explanation of facet indicators again and then select the correct answer to the question.

---

158 (164)

Your answer 2,33:7. No, this is wrong.

It is true that the , (comma) is the facet indicator for Personality. However, we said that this facet indicator is not used in a class number when the Personality isolate immediately follows the notation for its main class.

Please return to frame 164, read through the text again and then select the correct answer and continue with the course.

---

159 (153)

The concept 'university' appears as a focus in the Personality facet of Library science. You are right.

Class 2, Library science, is a good illustration of facet analysis in CC as all three facets, Personality, Matter and Energy are present. It is particularly convenient therefore for our present purposes.

The foci in the Personality facet are all *kinds of library*. The term library does not actually appear in the schedule but each concept in this facet is a kind of library. Thus university here means university library, local means local or public library.

The Matter facet, M, consists of *materials held in the library*. Under Foci in M you will see the instruction 'Same as Foci in P for Generalia Bibliography'. The isolates required have already been enumerated as the Personality facet of the Generalia Bibliography class and you will find them reprinted for you on frame 198 (CC page 2.29)—printed book, map periodical etc. When one of these isolate concepts is required as a Matter concept of Class 2 it is borrowed from this location in the schedules. This avoidance of unnecessary repetition in the listing of concepts is a feature of CC and of all faceted classification schemes.

The Energy facet, E, of class 2 consists of *operations carried out in the library*. Such activities or operations as cataloguing, classification and administration are listed here as Foci in E cum 2P.

At the side of each enumerated isolate is its ISOLATE NUMBER, ie the *notation* for that particular concept in that main.class. For example, university library has the notation, or isolate number 34 written in the schedule for class 2 as,

34 University

Continue on the next frame

---

160 (159)

If you consult our sample page from the *alphabetical index* to the CC schedules in frame 200 (CC page 2.169) under the term 'university' you will see first 2 [P], 34.

This tells you that 'university' occurs in class 2 (Library science) in the Personality facet, P, and has the isolate number 34 within that facet of that class.

This is followed by T [P], 4. This tells you that the concept 'university' *also* occurs in class T (Education) in the Personality facet P, with the isolate number, or notation, 4.

Now continue on frame 150.

---

161 (168)

You say that 234;14:55 is the correct class number. You are wrong.

The correct use of facet indicators is observed in this class number but you have not checked the schedules carefully enough to obtain the right *isolate number* for the concept 'maps'.

Look at the schedules again and you will see that your class number represents the subject of the document,

'The cataloguing of printed books in university libraries'

The correct class number should have been,

234;17:55

It is extremely important to check the schedules carefully and to work accurately with notation.

Please turn to frame 166 and continue with the course.

162 (167)
Your answer 234 571'N6. No, this is wrong.

You have not used any facet indicator for Space. There is thus nothing in this class number to show us that the notation 571 denotes the concept Sweden.

Please return to frame 166, read through the paragraphs on Space and Time facets again, then select another answer to the question.

---

163 (153)
You say that *'university'* is a focus in the Energy facet of class 2 Library science.

Foci in the Energy facet of a class are listed under the instruction *'Foci in (E) cum (2P)'*. You will not find the concept 'university' listed under this instruction within the schedule for Library science. It therefore does not belong to the Energy facet of this class.

Please return to frame 153. Read the question once more, check the schedule carefully and select another answer.

---

164 (150)
You say that 2:51 is the correct class number. You are right. Classification is an isolate within the Energy facet of Class 2 Library science. It is an Energy isolate. You have therefore used the : (colon) to introduce the isolate number from this facet.

The facet indicator for Personality is , (comma). This facet indicator is *not* used when the Personality isolate *immediately* follows the notation for its main class.

eg   Title   *'Classification in public libraries'*
                    MC   P   E
      SA   Library science/Public libraries/Classification
      Class number 22:51

In this example we have noted above each term in the subject analysis, (SA), the nature of the concept represented. MC means main class. This procedure is initially helpful when classifying by CC.

Look at the following example:

Title *'Reference services in college libraries'*
                MC   P   E
SA   Library science/College libraries/Reference service
Which is the correct class number?

2,33:7 – frame 158
233:7   – frame 168

165 (167)
Your answer 234'571.N6. No, you are wrong.

You have incorrectly used the facet indicators for Space and Time in this class number.

Please return to frame 166 and read through the paragraphs on Space and Time facets again. Then select another answer to the question and continue with the course.

---

166 (155, 161, 168)
Your answer 234;17;55. Good, this is correct. You have combined each element in the notation accurately.

We have briefly examined, and exemplified, P M and E facets and we must now consider Space and Time.

The concepts of Space and Time are the same in all subject areas. That is the same isolates play the same roles no matter what the subject. Consequently it would be wasteful and unnecessary to list, or enumerate, Space and Time facets in *every* main class schedule.

CC lists S and T facets *once only*.

Because these concepts are applicable for the subdivision of any area of knowledge they are often referred to in classification as *common subdivisions*.

Space isolate (CC pages 2.8 to 2.25)
We have reprinted a sample page from the CC Space isolate schedules on frame 196.

The majority of the CC Space isolate schedules consist of political divisions of the world. Each area is allocated a numerical notation, eg Africa 6, Union of South Africa 63, etc. This schedule has its own alphabetical index (beginning on CC page 2.18).

Space, S, has its own facet indicator just as P M and E do. In this case it is a full stop.

Thus Africa is expressed notationally as .6, the Union of South Africa as .63 and so on.
Continue on the next frame

167   (166)
Time isolate (CC page 2.7)
We have reprinted the entirety of the CC Time isolate schedule on frame
197. In the notation for Time, T, capital letters denote centuries and
certain geological periods and millenia. Individual decades and years are
specified numerically in a very simple way.

The facet indicator for T is ' (a single inverted comma). This is written
above the line as in quotation marks.

eg   1815 AD is expressed as   'M15
        20th century   'N
        the nineteen-forties   'N4
        1904 AD   'N04

Now consider the following document:

Title *Swedish university libraries in the 1960's*
                    MC   P   S   T
SA   Library science/University libraries/Sweden/1960s
Which is the correct class number for the subject of this document?
234 571 'N6   – frame 162
234.571'N6   – frame 170
234'571.N6   – frame 165

---

168   (164)
The correct class number is 233:7. Good. You are right. You have
correctly omitted the facet indicator for P in this case and have used
the correct facet indicator for E. Now try another example

Title *'Map cataloguing in university libraries'*
                    MC   P   M   E
SA   Library science/University libraries/Maps/Cataloguing
Which is the correct class number?
        234;14:55   – frame 161
        233;17:55   – frame 155
        234;17:55   – frame 166

---

169   (150)
Your answer 2;51. This is incorrect.

You have not observed the correct use of facet indicators in the construction of your class number.

The facet indicator you have used is ; (semi-colon). This is reserved
to introduce a concept from a *Matter* facet.

Classification does *not* occur as an isolate in the Matter facet of class 2
Library science. It is not therefore introduced by the ; (semi-colon).

Please return to frame 150. Read through the explanation of facet
indicators again and then select the correct answer to the question.

Your answer 234.571'N6. Correct. You have observed the correct use of the facet indicators . (full stop) for S and ' (single inverted comma) for T.

Form concepts
Like Space and Time the concepts of Form, although not influencing the *subjects* of documents, are applicable to all areas of knowledge.
In CC form concepts are also listed only once. In fact CC calls these isolates *'common isolates'*.

The treatment of form concepts is not altogether satisfactory in the 6th edition of CC and the relevant schedules certainly appear complex and somewhat confusing at first. As we are only concerned with the most important principles underlying CC, it is not worthwhile considering in detail the provisions which the scheme makes for these concepts.

(For the benefit of those readers who possess a copy of the scheme it should be noted that the schedules for form concepts are to be located in Chapter 02 page 2.3 *Book Number* and Chapter 2 pages 2.5 and 2.6 *Common Isolate*.)

All that we need to say here is that, when the classifier needs to specify form, either physical form or form of presentation, the appropriate concept is selected from the relevant schedule and is applicable to *any* main class within the scheme.

Unlike P M E S and T, concepts of form do not have any notation allocated as a facet indicator in CC.

For example, the form of presentation dictionary has the notation *k*. It would be used as follows:

Title	*A dictionary of geography*		
	MC	Form	
SA	Geography/Dictionary		
Class no	Uk		

or again,

Title	*A dictionary of child psychology*		
	MC	P	Form
SA	Psychology/Child/Dictionary		
Class no	Slk		

It is not necessary to pursue the mechanics of using form subdivisions any further at this stage.
Continue on the next frame

Before we go on to consider the process of synthesis in CC in more detail it would be useful to review briefly the main points made so far concerning this scheme.

SUMMARY

1   CC is an *analytico-synthetic* classification with a fully *faceted structure.*

2   CC does *not* enumerate compound subjects.

3   In the schedule of each main class only isolate concepts are enumerated.

4   These isolates, representing the phenomena studied by subject areas, are grouped into P M and E facets.

5   S and T isolates are listed only once.

6   Form isolates are listed only once.

7   It is the task of the indexer first to *analyse* the subjects of documents into their elementary constituents and then to *recombine*, or *synthesize,* these from the CC schedules.

8   The resulting expression of the subject of a document in notational terms constitutes the *class mark* or *class number* of that document.

Continue on the next frame

SECTION 3: ELEMENTS OF PRACTICAL CLASSIFICATION/PART II

Synthesis in classification is the process of combining concepts to produce a single statement of a compound subject. You have already employed the mechanics of synthesis in the construction of compound class numbers in CC.

When a compound subject consists of a basic subject and *2 or more* isolates, there arises the problem of deciding in what *order* the isolates should be combined in the single statement of that compound.

The order in which concepts are combined in compound subjects is called the *COMBINATION ORDER* or *CITATION ORDER*. It is of vital significance in classification and in subject indexing generally.

Citation order is exemplified in such a document as *'Cataloguing in university libraries'*. The subject analysis of this document would be

Library science/University libraries/Cataloguing.

We have here a basic subject, library science, and two isolates, *university libraries* and *cataloguing*. There are two possible citation orders for the isolate concepts in this compound subject, namely

1 Library science/University libraries/Cataloguing

or

2 Library science/Cataloguing/University libraries.

Citation order is thus a way of viewing the operation of *dividing* a class by the successive application of characteristics of division, only one characteristic being applied at each step in the division. Each step of division therefore represents a facet of a class.

Continue on the next frame

---

173 (172)

The problem of deciding on a citation order within the class Library science is the problem of deciding in what order the facets of this class should be applied in its subdivision.

If we initially consider only two facets of this class—Library and Operation—we have two possible citation orders for these facets, namely,

1 Library science/Library/Operation

or

2 Library science/Operation/Library

In the compound subject of the document *'Cataloguing in university libraries'* the citation order of concepts decided upon is,

Library science/University libraries/Cataloguing

Which citation order of facets does this represent?

Library science/Operation/Library   — frame 186
Library science/Library/Operation   — frame 180

174 (186)

No, you have just repeated the same mistake.

You must be clear in your mind about the existence of citation order before you go on to examine its implications.

Please return to frame 172 and read through the text again. Then attempt the questions once more.

---

175 (189)

You say that the subject analysis Library science/Administration/Canada/ Public libraries conforms to the citation order of PMEST. Consider your answer more carefully and you will see this is not so.

In the CC analysis of the class Library science, 'administration' is an Energy, [E], isolate, 'Canada' is a Space, [S], isolate and 'public library' is a Personality, [P], isolate.

Your answer therefore represents facets cited in the order,
Energy/Space/Personality.

This does not conform to the citation order PMEST.

Try another example within class 2, Library science.

Title: *'Cooperation between university libraries in Gt Britain in the 1960s'*

Which of the following subject analyses of this document is cast in PMEST citation order?

Library science/Cooperation/Gt Britain/
University libraries/1960s   — frame 188

Library science/University libraries/
Cooperation/Gt Britain/1960s   — frame 179

Library science/University libraries/
Gt Britain/Cooperation/1960s   — frame 190

176 (185)
Your answer 2:33,7.572. No, this is wrong.

The answer exhibits a misuse of facet indicators.

You have introduced a Personality concept by an Energy indicator : (colon) and an Energy concept by a Personality indicator , (comma).

Although the isolate numbers for the concepts are correct, these mistakes in the use of facet indicators render this class number meaningless. It is important to remember that precision in translation is vital. Apparently minor errors in the use of notational symbols can make nonsense of class numbers or make them express subjects you did not intend.

In this particular case our analysis was,

	P	E	S

Library science/College libraries/Reference services/Denmark producing the following CC class number:

233:7.572

Note that we do not require the Personality facet indicator for the introduction of concept college libraries. This is because it represents a *first level* Personality concept in class 2 Library Science and we do not use the facet indicator for first level personality.

Now please turn to frame 193 and continue with the course.

---

177 (188)
Your answer: Library science/Public libraries/Administration. Correct.

This conforms to the citation order of *facets* in the class Library science of

Library science/Library/Operations.

Please turn to frame 180 where you will go on to examine the significance and implications of citation order.

---

178 (181)
You say that the concept 'radiotherapy' would *not* constitute a distributed relative in the class Medicine. This is wrong.

Radiotherapy is a method of *treating* diseases and therefore belongs to the *'Treatment of disease'* facet of Medicine.

We said that this facet appears *third* in the citation order. It automatically follows that any concept belonging to this facet *will* constitute a distributed relative.

Please turn to frame 180 and read through the explanation of the relationship between citation order and distributed relatives again. Then select the correct answer to the question.

179 (175, 192)

Your answer, Library science/University libraries/Cooperation/Gt Britain 1960s.

Good, you are right. This conforms to the citation of facets in the order PMEST.

In this example, only *four* facets of the class Library science are manifest in the compound subject of the document.

These are P, E, S and T, cited in that order and represented by the concepts,

<pre>
        P   E   S   T
</pre>

University libraries/Cooperation/Gt Britain/1960s

Now please turn to frame 182 and continue with the course.

---

180 (173, 177)

You say that, in this instance, the citation order of facets in the class Library science is Library/Operation. You are quite right.

The concept University libraries belongs to the Library facet of Library science, Cataloguing is a concept in the Operations facet. The citation order of facets is therefore Library/Operation.

The significance of citation order may be illustrated by considering its implications for the classified arrangement of documents on the shelves.

Consider again the class Library science. All documents about Library science will be grouped together under this subject area, or main class if you like. The further subdivision of the documents within this class will be dependent upon the citation order employed in their classification.

Let us suppose the citation order of facets is Library/Operation. This will result in all the documents about a particular *kind of library* being grouped together. For example, documents about cataloguing in university libraries, management of university libraries, book-selection in university libraries etc, will all be located together, along with any other documents about university libraries.

Conversely, documents about a particular *operation* will be scattered, or dispersed. Documents on cataloguing in university libraries will *not* be grouped with documents about cataloguing, but with other documents about university libraries, cataloguing in public libraries with other documents about public libraries etc.

Thus, in order to retrieve *all* information about *cataloguing* the searcher would have to look in several different places. The same would apply to any other operation in Library science.

Classification groups together like concepts. By observing one characteristic of division at each grouping, the inevitable corollary of this, in the case of compound subjects, is that some concepts are *scattered* through their subordination to others.

Continue on the next frame

The citation order of concepts, reflecting the order of division, decides which concepts are grouped and which are successively scattered.

Only the concepts in the facet cited *first* in citation order will be grouped intact. In the above instance in Library science these concepts would be kinds of library. All the documents about a particular kind of library would be located in one place.

All the concepts in the second cited facet will be liable to scattering. In our example this means any operation in Library science.

As we proceed down the citation order, the concepts in each successively cited facet are liable to an increasingly higher degree of scatter.

These concepts, which, although 'related', are scattered, or 'distributed', by virtue of the citation order, are called *DISTRIBUTED RELATIVES*.

In the above example cataloguing is a concept in the Operations facet of Library science. Because this is not the first cited facet, cataloguing would constitute a *distributed relative* in the Library science class.

Consider the class Medicine. Suppose we have three facets which are cited in the following order,

	1	2	3

Medicine/Part of body/Disease/Treatment of disease

Given this citation order, which of the following concepts would *not* constitute a distributed relative in the class Medicine?

Radiotherapy — frame 178
Tuberculosis — frame 187
Heart — frame 189

Your answer, Library science/Public libraries/Administration/Canada. Correct. This conforms to the citation of facets in the order PMEST.

In this example, only three facets of the class Library science are manifest in the compound subject. These are P, E and S, cited in that order and represented by the concepts Public libraries, Administration and Canada respectively.

Having cited the isolate concepts present in the subject analysis in PMEST order, the indexer can then translate these into CC notation to produce the class number for the document.

eg Title	'Administration of Canadian public libraries'			
	MC	P	E	S
SA	Library science/Public libraries/Administration/Canada			
Class no	22:8.72			

Continue on the next frame

It has been stressed, as one of the basic precepts of CC, that there are only five Fundamental Categories of isolate concepts. You have seen how classes are analysed into facets which are named according to the Fundamental Categories and cited in PMEST order.

Now it is obvious that a subject area may well have *more* then just five facets. It might possess more than one Personality facet or more than one Energy facet etc.

The fact that the Fundamental Categories may manifest themselves more than once in a subject area is provided for, and systematized, in CC by further analysis into *ROUNDS* and *LEVELS* of P, M and E facets.

It is quite common for a class to possess more than one *level* of Personality. Take, for example, class I Botany (page 2.57).

The Personality, [P], facet of this class consists of *Plants*. Concepts which denote *parts of a plant*, eg leaf, flower, etc, are also Personality concepts. These constitute the *Organ* facet which is the second *LEVEL* Personality facet of this class or [P2].
(You will find the isolates of the [P2] facet enumerated on page 2.60 under the instruction 'Foci in [P2]'.)

The analysis of the document 'The study of the cellular structure of fungi' would be as follows,

     MC   P   P2

    Botany/Fungi/Cells

In this instance 'fungi' belongs to the [P] facets, *Plants*, and 'cells' to the [P2] facet, *Organ*, (ie part of the plant). They are cited in that order, which conforms to the order PMEST.

In some classes you will find third and even fourth levels of Personality, for example, class 0, Literature. In this class the facet structure is

     MC   P   P2   P3   P4

   Literature/Language/Form (ie literary form)/Author/Work

Now these *levels* of Personality, so far mentioned, would all be cited before any appearance of an Energy facet.

The first appearance of Energy can, however, be followed by a second *ROUND* of facets.

Consider the document *'The use of radiotherapy in the treatment of cancer of the stomach'*. This would be summarized as,

     MC   P   E   2E

   Medicine/Stomach/Cancer/Radiotherapy

In the analysis of class L, Medicine, 'stomach' is a concept in the Personality facet, [P], *Organ*, 'cancer' is a disease and as such appears in the Energy facet, [E], *Processes*, 'radiotherapy' is another Energy concept, appearing in another Energy facet, *Treatment of diseases*.

The *Treatment of diseases* facet follows the *Processes* facet, which includes diseases themselves, in the citation order for Class L.

Thus the *Treatment of diseases* facet appears *after* the first Energy facet, *Processes*. It is a second *ROUND* Energy facet, written as [2E].
Continue on the next frame

---

184 (183)
This idea of *ROUNDS* and *LEVELS* of P, M and E facets can, theoretically, be extended as far as is necessary in the facet analysis of a subject area.

You do not need to concern yourselves with the mechanics of using rounds and levels in classifying by CC.

It is only necessary for you to realize that these are the ways in which the scheme provides for the fact that subject areas, and therefore the compound subjects of documents do have more than just five facets, but that no matter how many facets are manifest, their isolates will always be P M E S or T isolates.

It is much more important to remember that the citation order of facets is *always* PMEST or, more precisely, PMErecurringST (PME...ST). The indexer has no choice in deciding the citation order of facets when classifying by CC. The citation order PME...ST is *prescribed*.
Continue on the next frame

---

185 (184)
The analysis into PMES and T facets applies, of course, to the phenomena studied by discipline.

Concepts of Form appear after [T], that is *last*, in citation order. Because they do not influence the subjects of documents, they are the least important concepts as regards grouping in classified order.

Conversely, it is important to keep information on [P] concepts grouped intact within their respective classes. They are thus cited first.

For example, the document '*A government report on the education of the physically handicapped in Great Britain*' would be summarized in the following PMEST citation order:

$$P \qquad\qquad S \qquad Form$$
Education/Physically handicapped/Gt Britain/Report

Within the basic class Education, physically handicapped is a concept from the [P] facet, persons receiving education. This is followed by the Space concept Great Britain and, finally, we have the form of presentation concept, report.

Now let us return to the Library science class and try a *translation* of a subject analysis in PME...ST citation order into a CC class number.

Title: '*A study of reference services in Danish college libraries*'

$$P \qquad\qquad\qquad E \qquad\qquad S$$
SA: Library science/College libraries/Reference services/Denmark

Consult the extracts from the CC schedules at the end of this book and decide which is the correct translation of the above subject analysis.

    2,33:7.572   — frame 191
    2:33,7.572   — frame 176
    233:7.572   — frame 193

---

186 (173)

You say that the citation order of facets is Library science/Operation/Library. No, this is wrong.

We cited the concepts present in the order, Library science/University libraries/Cataloguing.

Now the concept 'university libraries' belongs to the *Library* facet of Library science, and 'cataloguing' to the *Operations* facet.

Thus the citation order of *facets* is,

    Library science/Library/Operation.

Suppose you wish to apply this citation order of facets in classifying the document *'The administration of public libraries'*. In which of the following citation orders would the concepts appear?

    Library science/Administration/Public libraries   — frame 174
    Library science/Public libraries/Administration   — frame 177

---

187 (181)

You think that the concept 'tuberculosis' would *not* constitute a distributed relative in the class Medicine. No, you are wrong.

Tuberculosis is a *disease* and therefore belongs to the *'Disease'* facet of Medicine.

We said that this facet appears *second* in the citation order. It immediately follows from this that any concept belonging to this facet *will* constitute a distributed relative.

Please return to frame 180 and read through the explanation of the relationship between citation order and distributed relatives again. Then select the correct answer to the question.

---

188 (175, 192)

No. This answer is wrong.

You are still failing to distinguish between P M E S and T isolates and therefore you are unable to arrive at the correct citation order.

Please return to frame 175 and attempt the question again.

This time look *carefully* at the schedule for class 2, Library science. It will help you to recognize the facets present in the subject analysis and to arrive at a P M E S T citation order.

189 (181)

Your answer: 'heart' is the concept which would *not* constitute a distributed relative. Good. You are correct.

Heart is a concept in the *Part of body* facet of Medicine. In our example, Part of body is the *first cited facet* in this class. Consequently, the concepts within this facet would *not* be scattered, or distributed.

The problem posed by the inevitable occurrence of distributed relatives is one of the central problems of classification. It arises in the classified arrangement of documents and in the arrangement of subject catalogues. The decision as to citation order, which controls the degree to which any concept is distributed, is thus an extremely important one.

Let us return to CC with its analysis of facets into P M E S and T categories.

In CC, the citation order of facets in *ALL* main classes is the order
Personality   Matter   Energy   Space   Time
or
P M E S T

Whichever facets are found to be manifest in the subject analysis of a particular document, they are cited in the order P M E S T.

You have already examined the facet structure of class 2, Library science, in CC, and the kind of isolate concepts present in each of its facets.

Consider the following document,

Title: *'Administration of Canadian public libraries'*

Which of the following subject analyses of this document is cast in the citation order of P M E S T facets?

Library science/Administration/Canada/Public libraries — frame 175
Library science/Canada/Administration/Public libraries — frame 192
Library science/Public libraries/Administration/Canada — frame 182

---

190 (175, 192)

No. This answer is wrong.

You are still failing to distinguish P M E S and T isolates and therefore you are unable to arrive at the correct citation order.

Please return to frame 175 and attempt the question again. This time look carefully at the schedule for class 2. It will help you to recognize the facets present in the subject analysis and to arrive at a P M E S T citation order.

191 (185)
Your answer 2,33:7.572. No, this is not quite right.

You have inserted a , (comma) which is the Personality facet indicator, when it is not required.

It is true that 'college library' is a Personality concept in class 2 with the isolate number 33.

It is, however, a *first level* Personality and in such cases we do not need to use the Personality facet indicator.

The translation of the subject analysis
<pre>
                    P   E   S
</pre>
Library science/College libraries/Reference services/Denmark
should therefore be
    233:7.572

You should remember that precision is vital when translating into notational symbols. Even an apparently minor mistake can render a class number meaningless or give it a meaning you do not intend.

Please turn to frame 193 and continue with the course.

---

192 (189)
You say that the subject analysis Library science/Canada/Administration/ Public libraries conforms to the citation order PMEST. Look at this answer again and you will see it is incorrect.

In the CC analysis of the class Library science, 'Canada' is a Space, [S], isolate, 'administration' is an Energy, [E], isolate and 'public library' is a Personality, [P], isolate.

Your answer therefore represents facets cited in the order,
    Space/Energy/Personality

This *does not* conform to the citation order PMEST.

Try another example within class 2, Library science.
    Title: *'Cooperation between university libraries in Gt Britain in
       the 1960s'*

Which of the following subject analyses of this document is cast in PMEST citation order?

Library science/Cooperation/Gt Britain/ University libraries/1960s	– frame 188
Library science/University libraries/ Cooperation/Gt Britain/1960s	– frame 179
Library science/University libraries/ Gt Britain/Cooperation/1960s	– frame 190

193   (176, 185, 191)

Your answer: 233:7.572. Good, you are right. You have remembered the correct use of facet indicators in the construction of class numbers, and have cited the concepts in the correct order.

The facet analysis in CC all takes place within the context of main classes—ie areas of study or disciplines—these being the scheme's primary divisions of knowledge.

During the subject analysis of a document it is therefore essential to distinguish clearly between the area of study to which the subject belongs and the phenomena being studied.

The area of study so distinguished will give you the main class of the scheme within which framework all subsequent analysis and synthesis takes place.

In terms of CC analysis, your area of study may form a *canonical class*. You will remember that these were mentioned at the beginning of this section. In these cases your analysis and synthesis simply takes place within the canonical class which has its own facet structure.

Continue on the next frame

---

194   (193)

We shall now summarize the stages of work in the practical classification of a document from subject analysis to translation.

They have obvious relevance to practical classification using CC, and it is for this reason that the scheme is used to introduce the concepts and procedures involved in this subject.

They do, however, have equal validity for practical classification with any other scheme.

Stages in the practical classification of a document

1 *Subject analysis (specific summarization)*
   i) Decide on the area of study (discipline) to which the document belongs.
   ii) Cast the isolate phenomena present into the citation order PME...ST. At this stage the indexer is working in the *IDEA PLANE* of classification.

2 Locate the concepts expressed in the subject analysis in the schedules of the classification scheme, ie in the controlled vocabulary of indexing terms.

   This may be done at first by using the alphabetical index to the schedules. As familiarity with the scheme grows, it may be done by direct examination of the main class schedule in question.

   Never rely solely on the index, always examine the schedule. At this stage the indexer is working in the *VERBAL PLANE* of classification.

3 *Translation*
The concepts, located verbally in the schedules, must be translated
into the notations allocated to them.
     At this final stage the indexer is working in the *NOTATIONAL
PLANE* of classification.
Continue on the next frame

---

195 (194)
We are not going to proceed any further with our examination of subject
analysis and translation into CC. As a concluding exercise, therefore, it
would be helpful for you to try some examples of analysis and translation
on your own.
     The following examples are all drawn from Library science in order
that you can construct your CC class numbers by reference to our printed
extracts from the schedules.
     For each example you should produce:
          i) a subject analysis at the level of a specific summarization in a
               PME...ST citation order.
         ii) a translation of this analysis into a CC class number.
     Answers are provided on frame 201 against which you can check your
own solutions on completion.
     For your convenience we repeat here the CC facet indicators:
          Personality , (comma)
          Matter   ; (semi-colon)
          Energy   : (colon)
          Space   . (point)
          Time   ' (single inverted comma)

Examples
          1 Classification in the 1970s
          2 The management of research libraries in the USSR
          3 The cataloguing of filmstrips
          4 Hospital libraries in Sweden
          5 The use of periodicals in government libraries.
Turn to frame 201 for answers.

56487	Tyrone	643	Angola
56488	Londonderry	65	West Africa
57	Scandinavia	653	French West Africa
571	Sweden	654	Nigeria
572	Denmark	655	Ashanti
573	Norway	656	Liberia
574	Iceland	657	Ghana
575	Finland	658	Gambia
58	Russia	6591	Sierra Leone
591	Turkey	661	Rio de Oro
59191	Cyprus	663	Morocco
592	Balkan States	671	Algeria
5921	Rumania	673	Tunisia
5922	Bulgaria	674	Libya
5923	Yugo-slavia	677	Egypt
5925	Czecho-slovakia	6771	Sinai
5927	Albania	678	Sudan
5931	Austria	681	Eritrea
5932	Hungary	682	Abyssinia
594	Switzerland	683	British Somaliland
595	Poland	685	Italian Somaliland
596	Netherlands	687	Kenya
5961	Belgium	688	Uganda
5962	Holland	69	Islands
5966	Luxemberg	691	Madagascar
5971	Lithuania	692	Socotra
5973	Latvia	693	Mauritius
5975	Esthonia	698	Zanzibar
6	Africa	7	America
611	Tanganyika	71	North America
612	Mozambique	7191	Greenland
613	Rhodesia	72	Canada
		7211	Nova Scotia
6133	Southern Rhodesia	7212	New Brunswick
615	Nyasaland	722	Ontario
		723	Manitoba
63	Union of South Africa	724	Saskatchewan
631	Transvaal	7251	Alberta
632	Natal	7252	British Columbia
633	Orange Free State	7253	Yukon
634	Cape of Good Hope	726	North West Territory
		728	Quebec
641	Belgian Congo	7291	Prince Edward Islands
642	South West Africa	7292	Newfoundland

CHAPTER 3

TIME ISOLATE

31 Isolate in [T]: Chronological Division

A	Before 9999 B C	K	1600 to 1699 A D
A1	Eozoic	L	1700 to 1799 A D
A2	Palaeozoic	M	1800 to 1899 A D
A3	Mesozoic	N	1900 to 1999 A D
A4	Cainozoic	P	2000 to 2099 A D
A5	Quarternary	Q	2100 to 2199 A D
		R	2200 to 2299 A D
B	9999 to 1000 B C	S	2300 to 2399 A D
C	999 to 1 B C	T	2400 to 2499 A D
D	1 to 999 A D	U	2500 to 2599 A D
		V	2600 to 2699 A D
E	1000 to 1099 A D	W	2700 to 2799 A D
F	1100 to 1199 A D	X	2800 to 2899 A D
G	1200 to 1299 A D	YA	2900 to 2999 A D
H	1300 to 1399 A D		
I	1400 to 1499 A D	YB	3000 to 3099 A D
J	1500 to 1599 A D	YC	3100 to 3199 A D

32 Isolate in [T2]: Featured Time

c	Day-time	n5	Autumn
d	Night	n7	Winter
e	Twilight		
		p	Meteorological period
n	Season	p1	Dry
n1	Spring	p5	Wet
n3	Summer	p8	Snow

2·7

GENERALIA BIBLIOGRAPHY

a [P], [P2] [P3], [P4]

Foci in [P]

1	**By mode of production**
11	Tablet
12	Manuscript
128	Archive
13	Sound book
14	Printed book
15	Photo-reproduction
151	Micro
1511	Film strip
1512	Film roll
152	Photostat
17	Map
18	Raised type
2	**By script**
	(*To be divided by language*)
3	**By language**
	(*To be divided by language*)
4	**By nature of publication**
43	Book (conventional)
44	Newspaper
45	Recreative
46	Periodical
47	Reference book
48	Patent
494	Thesis
4994	Not-written book
4995	Book written but not existing
5	**By agency of production**
54	University
55	Government
58	Private
6	**By age of publication**
61	Old
66	Current
7	**By edition**
71	First
74	Proscribed
75	De luxe
77	Autograph
8	**By social group of readers**
	(*To be divided as in* Y *Sociology*)
95	**Translation**
	(*To be divided first by the language of the original and then by the language of the translation. A hyphen should be inserted between the two language numbers*)
991	**By size**
9911	Oversize
9912	Miniature
9917	Pamphlet

Foci in [P2]

1	List of publications in a geographical area
2	Library catalogue
3	Publisher's catalogue
4	Bookseller's catalogue
5	Catalogue of exhibition
7	Reading list

Foci in [P3] *and* [P4]

See Chapter 9a of the Rules

LIBRARY SCIENCE

2 [P]; [M]: [E] [2P]

Foci in [P]

1	**Trans-local**
11	World
13	Nation
14	Region
15	State
16	Division
2	**Local**
21	District
22	City
3	**Academical**
31	Elementary school
32	Secondary school
33	College
34	University
36	Research
4	**Business**
42	Industry
44	Newspaper office
45	Commerce
48	Government department

Others by (**SD**)

(*Illustrative*)

4(Q)	Religious
4(X81)	Insurance
5	**Subscription**
6	**Special class**
61	Child

63	Prisoner
64	Hospital
65	Woman
68	Blind
695	Seafarer
95	**Contact**
97	**Private**

Foci in [M]

Same as *Foci in* [P] for

Generalia Bibliography

Foci in [E] *cum* [2P]

1	Book selection
2	Organisation
3	Function
4	Co-operation
5	**Technical treatment**
51	Classification
55	Cataloguing
6	**Circulation**
61	Consultation
62	Lending
7	Reference service
8	**Administration**
81	Book Selection
811	Source
815	Indent
82	Order
84	Accession
85	Preparation
88	Maintenance
97	Documentation

2·30

201 (195)
Answers to examples set in frame 195.

                  E   T
1   Library science/Classification/1970s
         2:51'N7

                  P   E   S
2   Library science/Research libraries/Management/USSR
         236:8.58

                  M   E
3   Library science/Filmstrips/Cataloguing
         2;1511:55

                  P   S
4   Library science/Hospital libraries/Sweden
         264.571

                  P   M
5   Library science/Government libraries/Periodicals
         248;46

    The most important element in the above exercise is the subject analysis. Ensure that you have named all the required concepts at that specific level and have cited these in a PME...ST order.

    Providing you have achieved this, your translations will most likely be accurate. You may have had some difficulty locating the concepts in the schedule extracts but this difficulty would soon be overcome with increasing familiarity with a full schedule of classification and alphabetical subject index.

Continue on the next frame

---

202 (201)
You havenow completed this section of the course. The concepts and pro-cedures of subject analysis dealt with are applicable to all areas of know-ledge. The elements of practical classification, demonstrated by reference to Colon, are relevant to the use of all classification schemes.

    We do not pretend to have equipped you with an instant expertise in the subject analysis and classification of documents. We have, however, tried to provide you with a framework within which you can proceed to practice these techniques with a better understanding and therefore with increasing effectiveness.

Continue on the next frame

SECTION 4: UNIVERSAL DECIMAL CLASSIFICATION/PART I

In this section of the course you will be introduced to the Universal Decimal Classification which will be referred to throughout as the UDC. This is the scheme you will use for the remainder of your practical classification.

This section is intended to provide you with basic instruction and practice in the use of UDC as an indexing language for the classification of documents at the level of summarization.

The first edition of UDC was published in 1905. It was initially intended for use in the classified arrangement of a grandiose index to all recorded human knowledge, a 'universal index'. To this end it was developed by two Belgians, Paul Otlet and Henri La Fontaine, using the Decimal Classification of Melvil Dewey as the basis for their new scheme.

The idea of the universal index eventually came to nothing, but the UDC found favour as a general classification scheme and continued to develop in its own right.

The Fédération Internationale de Documentation (FID) is the international body with overall responsibility for the revision and maintenance of UDC. This responsibility is vested in the Central Classification Committee of FID which works in cooperation with the numerous national committees of the member countries.

The first and second editions of UDC, 1905 and 1927-1933 respectively, were both in French. The third edition, commenced in 1934 and completed in 1952, appeared in German. In 1943 work was begun on a fourth edition, to be published in English

An abridged version of the full UDC schedules was first published in English in 1948 by the British Standards Institution, the official British editorial body for the scheme.

In this course you will be using the *3rd Abridged English Edition* of UDC. This was first published by the British Standards Institution in 1961 as *BS1000A:1961*. Make very certain that your copy of UDC is the *Abridged English Edition, 3rd Edition, Revised 1961*. All references in this course are made to this latest abridgement.

At this point, before you go on to use UDC, it might be helpful to make some comments regarding this scheme and the Colon Classification (CC). These may help to answer the question, often asked by students, 'Why bother to learn about Colon, if we are going to use UDC?'. CC and UDC are both *general* classification schemes. They both face the problems presented in attempting to provide a system for the classification of all areas of knowledge.

In CC you have a classification scheme which is based on precisely defined principles, and postulates, and which adheres strictly to these principles.

The UDC, in its basic structure, predates CC and, as we shall see, it lacks much of this latter scheme's consistency and predictability.

Ranganathan's research into classification theory and practice, much of which is incorporated in his Colon Classification, is of accepted basic value in modern classification. It is therefore justifiable, and helpful, to view UDC in terms of Ranganathan's analysis of the problems of classification.

It is, however, essential to keep the historical context of UDC firmly in mind when studying and using the scheme. The results of more recent research may well elucidate parts of the scheme and improve its use in practical classification, but, ultimately, it must be seen as an indexing language in its own right to be used within its own limitations.

Now turn to your copy of the Abridged English Edition of UDC (BS1000A:1961).

As a prelude to using the scheme, we will briefly outline the various sections of this book. You will find a contents list on page 2 of your copy.

Introductory material pp 3-9. On these pages you will find descriptive and explanatory notes regarding the scheme. It would be wise to delay reading these until you have had some experience in using the scheme.

Tables of auxiliaries pp 10-25. These are auxiliary schedules, available for use in classification in conjunction with the main schedules. You will be referred to them when appropriate.

Main tables pp 27-145. These constitute the main schedules of the classification scheme. Do not forget that the schedules you have in front of you are an *abridged* version of the full UDC schedules. A list of some of the other editions of UDC can be found at the end of the book on page 254.

Alphabetical index pp 147-253. This is the alphabetical index to the schedules of the classification.

First of all we will consider the main schedules or *'main tables'*, so turn to page 26 of the scheme where you will find an outline of the main divisions of these schedules.

Continue on the next frame

UDC divides the whole of knowledge initially into ten broad areas. Each of these ten divisions is allocated a notation of one digit, thus:

0 Generalities
1 Philosophy
2 Religion
3 Social sciences
4 Linguistics
5 Natural sciences
6 Applied sciences
7 The Arts
8 Literature
9 History and Geography

You will see these divisions, with their notations, printed in bold type on page 26. The notation for Generalities, 0, is omitted.

It is interesting to note that these ten divisions bear a certain correlation, admittedly only a broad one, with the idea of Fundamental Disciplines, mentioned earlier in this course. With the exceptions of 0 Generalities, which in this scheme does *not* represent a unified discipline, and 4, Linguistics, which we would not regard as a Fundamental Discipline, the other primary divisions show this broad correlation.

Each of the ten primary divisions is successively subdivided into more narrowly defined subject fields.

The outline on page 26 of the scheme presents the major subdivisions. Thus, within 3, Social sciences, you find such subdivisions as,

32   Political science
37   Education

Within 5, Natural sciences, there are

51   Mathematics
52   Astronomy
53   Physics

and so on.

We shall examine the further, and more detailed, divisions presented in the main tables in due course. First cast your mind back to our examination of CC.

You will recall that the primary divisions of knowledge within CC are referred to as the main classes of that scheme.

Each main class in CC is a traditionally recognized discipline, or area of study, such as Agriculture (class J) or Geography (class U).

In UDC, it is usual to call the *first ten divisions*, 0 Generalities, 1 Philosophy, 2 Religion etc, the *main classes* of the scheme.

The subdivision of these ten main classes, eg

02   Librarianship
32   Political science
61   Medical science

are *sub-classes* within the scheme.

You will see that many of these sub-classes, the ones just mentioned, for example, correspond to *main classes* in CC.

This is because the concept of a 'main class' is usually defined in the literature of classification in terms of the notational plane. That is, the main classes of a scheme are the primary divisions of that scheme *as expressed in its notation.*

If a classification scheme employed, say, capital letters, A, B, C, D, etc, as the notation for its main classes, it could provide conveniently for twenty-six main classes.

UDC is based on Melvil Dewey's Decimal Classification. The Decimal Classification uses arabic numerals, divided decimally, for its notation. This notation provides conveniently for *ten* main classes, 000, 100, 200 etc, to 900.

This basic structure of ten main classes is retained by UDC, although Dewey's three digit base for each main class is dropped.

Which of the following statements is true?

Each classification scheme defines its main classes in accordance with the Fundamental Disciplines.	— frame 209
Each classification scheme defines its own set of main classes.	— frame 213

205　(215)

Your answer 03(091).

No, you are repeating the same kind of mistake. You are still failing to distinguish between terms representing form concepts and the same terms representing subject concepts.

Please return to frame 211. Read through the text carefully and attempt the question again.

206 (219)

Your answer, 61 "17". Yes, this is the correct class number for the document *'Eighteenth century medicine'*.

Dates are expressed in UDC as numerical statements. Centuries are denoted by their *first two* digits only. The concept 'eighteenth century' or *'the 1700s'* is thus expressed as "17".

Space, or as UDC prefers, *Place*, concepts are listed in schedule (e) on pages 12-21. Turn now to this schedule.

The notations for Space concepts are enclosed in round brackets, ( ), and added to the main table numbers when required for the further subdivision of a class.

Political and *administrative* areas are enumerated for you in schedule (e)

    eg   (420)   England
            (423.8) Somerset

Physiographic divisions of the earth's surface are also enumerated

    eg   (22) Islands
            (23) Mountains

In addition, UDC provides for certain Space concepts such as *orientation.* These concepts are always used in conjenction with some other Space division, political or physiographic, and are introduced by - (hyphen).

    eg   'Coal mining in Somerset'   622.333(423.8)
          'Coal mining in north Somerset' 622.333(423.8-17)

Select the correct class number for a document about *'The folklore of the West Riding of Yorkshire'.*

    398(427.4-15)   – frame 227
    39 (427.4-15)   – frame 216
    398(427.415)   – frame 243

---

207 (228)

Your answer 663.93.047. Good. This is quite correct.

In order to denote the concept 'freeze-drying' you have used one of the special auxiliaries enumerated under 66.0.

Freeze-drying is denoted by the special auxiliary .047. It is introduced in a class mark by the facet indicator .0 (point nought).

Now please turn to frame 221 where you will find another example of the use of special auxiliaries.

208   (214)
You say that the correct class number is 611.2. You are wrong.

If you consult the alphabetical index under 'Respiratory system', 611.2 is one of the class numbers to which you are referred.

However, on checking the schedules, you can see that 611.2 is a subdivision of class *611 Anatomy*. It represents the *anatomy* of the respiratory system. The concept *disease* is *not* provided for in this class number.

Return to frame 214, select another answer to the question and this time check the context of the class number in the schedules carefully.

---

209   (204)
You say that each classification scheme defines its main classes in accordance with the Fundamental Disciplines. No, this is not true.

We did say that the main classes in UDC bear a broad correlation with the Fundamental Disciplines—Philosophy, Religion, Natural science, etc.

But what about CC?   Agriculture, Education, Economics, Political science are all *main classes* within this scheme but they are not Fundamental Disciplines.

Please return to frame 204 and read through what was said about main classes again. Then select the correct answer to the question and proceed with the course.

---

210   (214)
Your answer 616.2. Correct.

616.2 is a subdivision of class *616 Disease* and it specifies *respiratory diseases*.

In some cases, then, as in *'Diseases of the respiratory system'*, UDC provides the indexer with a ready-made class number for a compound subject.

This scheme does *enumerate* some compound subjects. In the above example you were able to find an enumerated class number in the main tables which provided an adequate translation of your subject analysis. No synthesis was required.

Unlike CC, UDC does not confine its enumeration to isolate concepts.

The enumeration of compound subjects is, however, limited. UDC recognizes, to a high degree, the value of *synthesis* in classification. In the great majority of cases you will employ some synthesis when classifying documents by this scheme.

There are many provisions within the scheme which allow for the synthesis of concepts in the notational expression of compound subjects.

We shall look first at the *COMMON AUXILIARIES*. These are located under the *Tables of auxiliaries* beginning on page 10. So turn now to this part of the scheme.

Continue on the next frame

The *COMMON AUXILIARIES* are so called because their schedules are *auxiliary* to the main tables and *common* in that they are available for the subdivision of *all* classes.

You have already used such 'common subdivisions' when providing for Space, Time and Forms concepts in CC.

Let us look first at the common auxiliaries of Form, schedule (d) on page 11 of the scheme.

The majority of this schedule is devoted to various *forms of presentation*,

    eg   (048)   Abstracts
          (083)   Formulae
Physical forms are also included,

    eg   (086.4) Globes and relief maps
          (086.7) Gramophone records, tapes
We may note that the concept of *intellectual form* is also provided for,

    eg   (091)   Historical presentation
The common auxiliaries of Form are identified in a class number by their own distinctive facet indicator (0...).

Remember, they are available for the subdivision of *any* class if required. You do *not* need to receive explicit instructions in the main tables indicating their availability.

Look, for example, at the way in which the class numbers for the following documents are derived by referring to the appropriate parts of the index and classified schedules.

    Title: *'A directory of civil engineering'*
    SA: Engineering/Civil/Directory
    Class no: 624(058.7)

    Title: *'A dictionary of psychology'*
    SA: Psychology/Dictionary
    Class no: 159.9(03)
As we said in the section of this course devoted to subject analysis, it is important to distinguish carefully between terms representing true *form* concepts and the *same* terms representing *subject* concepts.

Take, for example, a document titled *'A history of periodicals'*.

Which of the following is the correct class number for this document?

    93(051)   – frame 215
    05(091)   – frame 219

212 (215)

Your answer 93(03). Correct.

In this case, *'A dictionary of history'*, 'history' is the subject concept and 'dictionary' the form concept.

You have made the correct distinction in your subject analysis and translated accurately.

Please turn to frame 219 and continue with the course.

---

213 (204)

You say that each classification scheme defines its own set of main classes. Yes, this is quite true.

Main classes are thus only capable of *precise* definition in the contexts of particular classification schemes. That which constitutes a main class according to the notation of one scheme, does not necessarily constitute a main class in another scheme. This can be seen in a comparison of the main classes of CC and UDC.

There is, however, a tendency to employ the term 'main class' in the *idea plane* of practical classification. Thus, in the subject analysis of a document, the *discipline* to which a document belongs is often referred to as its 'main class'.

We have done this when working with CC, for, in that scheme, the discipline concepts recognized in subject analyses usually correspond *directly* to main classes in the schedules.

In our future subject analyses of documents, for the purposes of classification by UDC, we shall use the term *BASIC CLASS* to distinguish disciplines from phenomena studied by disciplines.

We shall reserve the term *main class* to denote structural divisions of particular classification schemes.

UDC, then, has ten main classes.

You have seen that these main classes, with the exception of 0 Generalities, represent discipline concepts. In several cases they correspond to Fundamental Disciplines.

At the first level of subdivision of most of the main classes, we find sub-classes which usually represent sub-disciplines.

Look at the schedule of main class *5, Mathematics and Natural sciences*, on page 59 of the scheme. You will see that the first major sub-class is *51 Mathematics.* On page 61 you will find class *52 Astronomy* followed by *53 Physics and Mechanics.*

Now carry on through the schedule for main class 5 and note the major sub-classes into which it is divided. Their headings are printed in bold type across the centre of the pages. You will see that each of these sub-classes constitutes a sub-discipline Geology, Botany etc.

The basic principle of UDC, as with CC, and all the major general classification schemes, is to classify documents *first* according to the disciplines to which they belong.

A word of warning is advisable at this early stage, however. There are very few principles in UDC which are applied *strictly* throughout the scheme. In this sense the scheme differs widely from CC.

UDC is essentially a pragmatic scheme and, in many instances, pragmatic decisions override classificatory principles. As you will see, this makes for a lack of consistency.

In many areas, the scheme allows a great deal of freedom to the indexer in its usage. This is in contrast to CC, which was the first major scheme to prescribe very precise rules as to its application.

Because of this degree of freedom, the indexer must formulate his own rules when applying UDC. Otherwise the situation would become chaotic.

In your practical classification with UDC you are going to employ as your guide some of the principles which we have already established as useful.

This is particularly so at the very important stage of the subject analysis of documents. As with CC, your subject analyses will be *specific summarizations* of the dominant theme of each document.

You are required to cast these analyses in the citation order PME...ST Form. The reasons for this will become increasingly clear.

To help you arrive at this order, and to help you identify P M and E isolates, you have been provided with the tables showing the categories and citation order in CC. The classes have been arranged in UDC order, that is in the order in which they appear in the UDC main tables. Do not forget to refer to this table in your practical classification; it is to be found in the Appendix.

Continue on the next frame

We will begin to classify by UDC at its level of least complexity. This will serve to introduce you to the alphabetical index to the schedules.

Suppose you have to classify the following document,

Title: *'The psychology of perception'*
SA: Psychology/Perception

Here you have a compound subject consisting of a basic class, psychology, and one isolate, perception.

Consult the alphabetical index under the term perception (page 216). You will see the following entry:

Perception. Cf Intuition; Sensory . . .
     occult 133.3

That part of the entry, *occult 133.3*, tells you that the concept perception occurs in the classified schedule at class number 133.3.

Turn to this part of the schedule (page 30). Perception appears here in main class 1, Philosophy in the context of 133 occultism. The subdivision 133.3 gives you, specifically, occult perception. You have decided, in your subject analysis, that this document belongs to the basic class Psychology. You do not wish to use perception in the context of occultism and therefore you reject this class number.

Return to your alphabetical index entry. That part of the entry, *Cf Intuition, sensory . . .* , tells you that you should also consider those entries under the terms *Intuition* and *Sensory* (perception).

Sensory perception appears to fit your particular context so consult this entry. Here you will see

Sensory perception   159.937
     animals   591.185

You do not want sensory perception *in animals*, so consult the schedules under 159.937 (page 31).

Here you find perception as a subdivision of class 159.93 Sensation. Sense perception which, in turn, is a subdivision of the class 159.9 Psychology.

You need go no further. Your desired class number, the translation of your subject analysis, is enumerated for you in the schedules, namely,

159.937

Remember, never classify by the alphabetical index alone. Always check the schedules to ensure that the desired concept is in the desired context.

Now take the following document:

Title: *'Diseases of the respiratory system'*
SA: Medicine/Respiratory system/Diseases

Which of the following is the correct class number?

616   — frame 218
611.2   — frame 208
616.2   — frame 210

215 (211)

You think that the correct class number is 93(051). No, you are wrong.

The document was titled *'A history of periodicals'*. In this case the term 'periodicals' represents the *subject* of the document. It is *about* periodicals. It is not itself a periodical.

In your class number 'periodicals' appears as a form concept, while 'history', which in this instance represents a concept of intellectual form, appears as the subject of the document.

Now try another example.

Which of the following is the correct class number for the document *'A dictionary of history'*?

  93(03)   — frame 212
  03(091)   — frame 205

---

216 (206)

You say that the class number is 39(427.4-15). No, this is wrong.

The class number is not *specific* enough for the subject of the document. Return to frame 206, check the index and the schedules for class 39 carefully before selecting another answer to the question.

---

217 (228)

Your answer 663.047. No, this is not correct.

This class number is not specific enough for the subject of the document. You have specified 'beverages' but not the particular beverage in question, coffee.

Please return to frame 228. Check the index and the schedule for class 663 carefully. Then select the correct answer to the question and proceed with the course.

---

218 (214)

Your answer 616. No, this is incorrect.

You might have arrived at this class number by consulting the alphabetical index under the term 'disease'.

616 *does* represent the concept disease, or pathology, in class 61 Medical sciences. But what about 'respiratory system', is this provided for in the class number 616? The answer is no.

Return to frame 214, select another answer to the question and check the class number carefully in the schedules.

219 (211)

Your answer 05(091). Correct.

In this case, *'A history of periodicals'*, the term 'periodicals' represents the *subject* of the document. As a subject concept it appears in the Generalities main class at 05. 'History' is the *form* concept, provided for in UDC as common auxiliary (091), historical presentation.

Let us now consider *Time* concepts. These are listed in schedule (g) of the common auxiliaries, page 22. The facet indicator for Time is " " (quotation marks).

Dates are expressed numerically and enclosed in quotation marks. Examples are provided in the notes to schedule (g) which you should read through. Here you will see illustrated the notations for individual days, years, decades and centuries. There is obviously no need to provide an exhaustive enumeration.

Certain aspects of Time which *do* require a specifically allocated notation are enumerated under *'Other time aspects'*, eg "313" Future.

Which of the following is the correct class number for the document *'Eighteenth century medicine'*?

61 "18"   — frame 229
61 "1800"   — frame 226
61 "17"   — frame 206

---

220 (234)

Your answer 351.741.082. Correct.

In order to denote the concept 'promotion' you have used the special auxiliaries enumerated at 35.07/.08. You have this time utilized the correct facet indicator .0 (point nought).

Please go on to frame 221 where you will find another example of the use of special auxiliaries.

---

221 (207, 220)

This time we wll try an example taken from the discipline Architecture.

The document is about *'Islamic architecture'*.

Which of the following is the correct class number for this document?

72.7.033.3   — frame 230
7.033.3   — frame 235
72.033.3   — frame 240

222 (241)

Your choice, 911.3:61(5). Yes, this is the correct class number for the document *'A medical geography of Asia'*. In this class number, the concept 'medicine' is taken from its location in class 61 and linked by the colon to 911.3, Human geography. Asia is provided for by the common auxiliary of Place, (5).

In class 911 you are *instructed* to divide by the rest of the classification, when required, using the colon.

You need not, however, receive these explicit instructions before you proceed to use this device. You are free to subdivide *any* class in UDC by any other appropriate part of the schedules in this manner, if this should be required.

If a concept is neither directly enumerated as part of a compound, nor provided as a special auxiliary of the class in which you are working, nor as a common auxiliary, it can be taken from any relevant part of the schedules in which it does occur.

We stress *relevant*. When 'borrowing' such a concept always check its precise context in the schedules to ensure that it is appropriate to your needs. Moreover, the *full* class number must always be used to ensure that this precise context is expressed.

Which of the following is the correct class number for the document *'The circulation of sap in cactuses'*?

582.85:631.577	– frame 232
582.85:581.112	– frame 245
582.85:1.112	– frame 242

---

223 (246)

You think that this represents a *compound* subject. No, you are wrong.

Earlier in this course we defined a compound subject as consisting, at the level of summarization, of a *basic subject and two or more of its isolates*.

The analysis of this document in question reveals another kind of element.

Please return to frame 246 and read through the explanation of phase relations again. Then consider the question once more and select the correct answer.

---

224 (244)

Your answer 546.13/546.14. No, you are not right in this.

You have attempted to aggregate the UDC class number incorrectly.

Please return to frame 244 and read again about the use of the / (oblique stroke), paying particular attention to the examples given. Then check the schedules carefully when selecting the correct answer to the question.

225 (244)

Your answer 546.13. This is incorrect.

The document in question is about *'The chemistry of chlorine and bromine'*.

Your class number denotes *'The chemistry of chlorine'*.

Return to frame 244 and read again about the aggregation of class numbers. Then select another answer to the question and proceed with the course.

---

226 (219)

Your answer 61 "1800". No, this is incorrect.

Dates are expressed *numerically* in UDC. You simply take the numerical statement of, say, a particular year and enclose this in " " (quotation marks). In other words, you have a ready-made notation, eg

    1066 AD   "1066"
    1972 AD   "1972"

If you wish to denote a century, you use the first *two digits* of that century's *numerical statement*, eg

    Twentieth century   "19"

Your class number denotes 'Medicine in the year *1800*', *not* 'Eighteenth century medicine'.

Please return to frame 219 and select the correct answer to the question.

---

227 (206)

Your answer 398(427.4-15). Right.

Yorkshire is specified as (427.4). If we wish to denote the *West Riding* of Yorkshire we use the notation (-15) for the concept *'west'*, hence (427.4-15).

We shall mention some of the other common auxiliaries of UDC in due course.

Remember that, like Space, Time and Form, *common auxiliaries* are available for the subdivision of *any* class when required.

You can, of course, use *more than one* common auxiliary if this is necessary in the specification of a subject.

    eg *'An encyclopaedia of the folklore of the West Riding of Yorkshire'*
       398(427.4-15)(03)

Continue on the next frame

So far you have seen two ways in which UDC provides for the classification of concepts.

    1 Direct enumeration of compound subjects in the main tables

    2 Provision of common auxiliaries

We are now going to look at a third method, the use of *SPECIAL AUXILIARIES.*

It was said earlier that the enumeration of compound subjects in UDC is restricted. The scheme employs the principle of synthesis to a high degree. The common auxiliaries allow for some synthesis but they are obviously insufficient by themselves. The special auxiliaries allow the process of synthesis to be taken one stage further.

In many of its classes, UDC lists certain concepts once only as *'special auxiliaries'* of that class. These special auxiliaries are available for the further subdivision of that class when required.

You are already familiar with the idea of enumerating isolate concepts in the rigorous facet analysis of CC. The special auxiliaries of UDC represent a less systematically developed use of facet analysis.

Special auxiliaries are identified by the facet indicators,

    - (hyphen)

and

    .0 (point nought)

There is also a restricted use of special auxiliaries introduced by ' (apostrophe) in parts of the Chemistry class which we need not pursue in this course. (See section (k) on page 25 of the scheme for explanatory notes on special auxiliaries.)

Special auxiliaries are listed in the main tables and are 'special' in the sense that their use is restricted to those classes of which they form an integral part.

You do not always receive explicit instructions in the schedules as to the exact extent of the applicability of these auxiliaries. In many cases this has to be inferred from the position in any given class.

Look, for example, at *class 3, Social sciences*, on page 36. Here you will see that the concepts in the *Persons* facet of class 3 are provided for by special auxiliaries enumerated at 3-05.

These auxiliaries can be applied *throughout* class 3 if required. They are *not* repeated in each of its sub-classes

    eg   *'Sociology of young people'*
          Sociology/Young people
          301-053.7

Now turn to *class 66 Chemical industry. Chemical technology*, on page 116.

Initially you receive the instruction

    66-2/-8 As 621-2/-8 plant, processes, product details.

This tells you that you may use the special auxiliaries already enumerated at 621-2/-8, and therefore not repeated here in full.

    eg   *'Safety installations in the manufacture of high explosives'*
             Technology/Chemical industry/High explosives/Safety
             installations
             662.2-781

At 66.0 you are provided with another set of special auxiliaries. These represent *Operations* and *Processes*. These are also available for use throughout class 66 and are enumerated at this point in the schedules.

Now consider a document about *'The freeze drying of coffee'*. We could summarize this as

        Technology/Drinks industry/Coffee/Freeze drying

Which of the following is the correct class number for this document?

663.93-047	– frame 234
663.047	– frame 217
663.93.047	– frame 207

---

229 (219)

Your answer 61 "18". No, this is incorrect.

We said that *dates* are expressed *numerically*. Centuries are denoted by the *first two* digits of their numerical statement.

"18" thus indicates the 1800s, or the *nineteenth century*.

Please return to frame 219 and select another answer to the question.

---

230 (221)

You say that the correct class number is 72.7.033.3. No, you are wrong.

The special auxiliaries to which you have recourse in this case are enumerated under 7.0.

These are available for use in class 72 Architecture, but you are *not* required to repeat the *entire* notation, eg 7.033.3, when subdividing class 72 by one of these special auxiliaries.

Please return to frame 221 and select the correct answer. Check its method of construction carefully in the schedules.

---

231 (241)

You say 911:61(5). No, this is wrong.

You have specified the concepts 'medical' and 'Asia' correctly. Class 911 is, however, subdivided into physical geography and human geography *before* the use of the colon is resorted to.

You have not observed these prior divisions in your class number but have 'coloned' directly to 911.

Please return to frame 241. Select the correct class number and check its construction carefully in the schedules.

232 (222)

You say 582.85:631.577. No, you are wrong.

On consulting the index under the term 'sap' you are referred to 631.577. However, it was said that you must always check the precise context of a concept *in the schedules* to ensure that it is appropriate to your needs.

Please return to frame 222 and select another answer to the question while remembering to observe this rule.

---

233 (246)

You think this represents a *simple* subject. You are wrong.

Earlier in this course we defined a simple subject as consisting, at the level of summarization, of *a basic subject and one isolate drawn from that area of knowledge*, eg Religion/Christianity.

The analysis of the document in question certainly produces more elements than these.

Please return to frame 246 and read through the explanation of phase relations again. Then consider the question once more and select the correct answer.

---

234 (228)

Your answer 663.93-047. No, you are wrong.

We said that there are two facet indicators for the special auxiliaries
- (hyphen)

and

.0 (point nought)

The facet indicator to be used for any particular special auxiliary is dictated in the schedules where that auxiliary is enumerated.

In this instance you are using the special auxiliaries enumerated at *66.0*. These auxiliaries are therefore introduced by .0 (point nought) *not* - (hyphen).

Now try another example.

The document is entitled *'Promotion of personnel in the police force'*. This is summarized as

Public administration/Public services/Police/Promotion

Which of the following is the correct class number?

351.741-082 — frame 239
351.741.082 — frame 220

235 (221)

You say that 7.033.3 is the correct class number. No, you are wrong.

This class number fails to denote the discipline concept Architecture. You have simply located the notation for the particular *special auxiliary* that you wish to employ.

Return to frame 221 and select the correct answer to the question.

---

236 (244)

Your answer 546.13/.14. Quite correct.

You have aggregated the class numbers for the concepts 'chlorine' and 'bromine' to produce the distinct class number 546.13/.14. In constructing this aggregate class number, you have rightly omitted a repetition of the digits 546 following the / (oblique stroke).

The + (plus sign) can be used for adding *non-consecutive* UDC class numbers.

In this way the indexer can link two or more concepts, associated in the literature but separated in the UDC schedule order.

When using the + (plus sign) the *full* class number for each concept is *always* used

      eg   *'The chemistry of chlorine and fluorine'*

           546.13+546.16

Construct a class number, using the + (plus sign), for the document *'Economic geology and mining in the USA'*. Then turn to frame 248.

---

237 (246)

You say that the document about *'The influence of religion on Renaissance art'* represents a complex subject. Correct.

The summarization of this document would be

      Art/Renaissance/*Influenced by*/Religion

This reveals a phase relation of the influence kind. As the subject includes a phase relation it is a *complex subject*.

In UDC we must rely on the : (colon) to indicate a phase relation. We cannot express the particular *kind* of phase relation existing.

The class number for this document is, consequently,

      7.034:2

Continue on the next frame

238　(237)

In certain classes UDC *instructs* the indexer to express a desired concept by a simple *VERBAL* statement.

Look, for example, at *class 8, Literature.* There is no author facet enumerated in this class. Individual authors are not allocated numerical notations.

If you wish to specify an individual author, you do so by simply writing his or her *name*, as instructed

    eg   *'The works of Charles Dickens'*   820 DICKENS
           'The poems of Lord Byron'   820.1 BYRON

You do not, however, need to receive instructions in the schedules before you may employ these *VERBAL EXTENSIONS* to UDC class numbers.

In any class, if a desired concept is not specified in the 'normal' UDC notation, it can be individualized by a verbal extension to the class number.

Verbal extensions are particularly useful when specifying individual persons, places, plants, animals etc, which are not specified in UDC notation.

Now consider the following document.

    Title *'A West Country village: Ashworthy: family, kinship and land'*

This can be summarized as:

    Social geography/England/West Country/Village communities/ Ashworthy

Construct a class number for this document using an appropriate verbal extension and then turn to frame 244.

239　(234)

Your answer 351.741-082. No, you are wrong.

You are still making the same mistake in that you are failing to use the correct facet indicator for the special auxiliary in question.

Return to frame 234. Read through the text and then select the correct answer to the question remembering to consult the schedules very carefully.

240 (221)
Your answer 72.033.3. Correct.

In class 72, Architecture, the *Style*, or *Period*, facet is provided for by special auxiliaries enumerated at 7.03 and applicable throughout main class 7.

Thus the class number for a document about 'Islamic architecture' is 72.033.3 in which .033.3 is the special auxiliary denoting 'Islamic style'.

As in most other aspects of UDC, there is no hard and fast rule which can be relied upon to predict the occurence of special auxiliaries. Analysis within the scheme is too inconsistent to allow for this.

Each class must be taken as a discrete case. In some the use of special auxiliaries is highly developed; in others non-existent.

Thus, when classifying a document, if a desired concept is not enumerated as part of a compound class number, look to see if it is provided for as a special auxiliary of the class in which you are working.
Continue on the next frame

---

241 (240)
We now come to the most powerful device for synthesis provided in UDC, the use of the relational sign : (colon).

By means of this device, any class in UDC can be subdivided by any other appropriate part of the scheme, should this be required in the expression of a compound subject. The notations for the concepts thus compounded are linked by the : (colon).

Look, for example, at class 911, General geography, on page 143 of the scheme.

General, or 'systematic', geography is a very wide-ranging area of study encompassing such diverse fields as geomorphology, economic geography, biogeography etc.

The concepts which define the particular *kind* of systematic geography, economic, cultural etc, can be regarded as the personality concepts of this class (see CC).

Now in UDC these concepts are not provided for as special auxiliaries of class 911. They do *not* fall within the province of the common auxiliaries, nor all they *all* directly enumerated in class 911 as compound subjects. The class is broadly subdivided into Physical geography, 911.2 and Human geography 911.3, which are thus provided for as directly enumerated compounds, but this enumeration does not go into sufficient detail.

Consequently, when one of these concepts is required in the further subdivision of class 911, it is 'borrowed' from another part of the main tables. It is taken from the appropriate class in which it *is* enumerated and linked by a colon to class 911.

You are, in fact, instructed to do this, and provided with examples, in the schedule for class 911, thus,

911.3   Human (cultural) geography. By :3..., :6..., etc.
       :32   Political geography   :33 Economic geography

The class number for *Political geography* is, then, *911.3:32*, in which the concept 'political' is taken from its location at class 32, Political science, and joined by the : (colon) to 911.3, Human geography.

According to the same principle, the class number for *Economic geography* is 911.3:33.

The use of the : (colon) in class 911 is a clear illustration of the principle of making the *whole of the classification scheme* available for the subdivision of any given class when required.

This principle is not unique to UDC. Both CC and the Dewey Decimal Classification employ it. In these schemes, however, the device is *only* used to specify the *species of a genus*, eg a particular *kind* of library such as medical or agricultural library.

Its use in UDC is far more widespread. It is the most important provision for synthesis within the scheme and has therefore to be relied upon in many situations. Its usage is less well defined than in either CC or Dewey and is certainly not restricted to the specification of the species of a genus.

Now consider the following document,
   '*A medical geography of Asia*'
Which of the following is the correct class number for this document?
   911:61(5)   – frame 231
   911.3:61:(5)   – frame 247
   911.3:61(5)   – frame 222

---

242 (222)
Your answer 582.85:1.112. No, this is wrong.

You must always use the *full* class number for any concept by which you are subdividing a class through the use of the : (colon).

If you do not observe this rule, the resulting class number will be either meaningless or, at least, have the wrong meaning.

Look at your class number again and you will see that it is meaningless. For what concept does the notation: 1.112 stand?

Return to frame 222 and select the correct answer to the question.

---

243 (206)
You say that the class number is 398(427.415). No, you are wrong.

You have incorrectly constructed that part of the class number which specifies the space concept 'West Riding of Yorkshire'.

Return to frame 206 and read what was said about Space concepts again. Then select the correct answer to the question and proceed with the course.

Your class number should be 308(423-202 Ashworthy) *or* 911.3:308(423-202 Ashworthy).

In the above example, when specifying the individual village, Ashworthy, we must employ a *verbal extension* to the 'normal' UDC notation.

All the devices which you have so far encountered—common cuxiliaries, special auxiliaries, use of the : (colon), verbal extensions—allow for the further *subdivision* of classes.

They thus allow for the *narrowing* of a given class.

UDC also allows the indexer to *widen* or *expand* the scope of a class. This is achieved through the use of two notational devices.

   / (oblique stroke)
   + (plus sign)

We shall consider first the / (oblique stroke). This is used for the linking of *consecutive* UDC class numbers. The result of this is to provide a distinct class number for an aggregate of subjects which are adjacent in the UDC schedule order.

   eg   5/6   Science and technology
        343/347   Criminal and civil law

Thus a document about *'Science and technology in the USSR in 1970'* would receive the class number 5/6 (47) "1970".

If the class numbers for the concepts so aggregated possess *the first three digits* in common, there is no need to repeat these digits following the / (oblique stroke).

   eg   Title   *'The importance of butter and cheese production in
                the agriculture of Southwest Ireland'*
        SA   Agriculture/Dairy produce/Butter and cheese/
                SW Ireland
        Class no 637.2/.3(417-14)

Now consider the following document, *'The chemistry of chlorine and bromine'*.

Which of the following is the correct class number?

   546.13/546.14   — frame 224
   546.13   — frame 225
   546.13/.14   — frame 236

Your answer 582.85:581.112. Good, this is quite correct.

Remember always to check the precise context of a concept 'borrowed' from another part of the main tables and used for the subdivision of a given class. This is to ensure that the context is appropriate to your needs.

Never classify by the index alone.

Remember always to express this context *in full* by adding the *full class number.*

If these procedures are not carefully observed, the resulting class number can be either meaningless, or, at least, not have the desired meaning.

It might be useful at this point to review briefly the procedures mentioned so far in the classification of documents by UDC.

SUMMARY

1 The subject of the document, as expressed in your subject analysis, may be directly enumerated in the main tables.

2 If this is not the case, the further concepts you wish to express may be provided for by a variety of ways involving synthesis in the notational plane. These are:

3 By means of a special auxiliary, or auxiliaries, applicable only as indicated in the schedules.

4 By means of a common auxiliary, applicable to all classes.

5 By means of the : (colon) which allows you further to divide the class in which you are working by any other relevant part, or parts, of the main tables.

Continue on the next frame

The concepts introduced by the : (colon) may be manifestations of either Personality, Matter or Energy facets within a given compound. Space and Time have their own distinctive facet indicators like all the common auxiliaries.

UDC calls the colon a 'relational' sign and indeed it is. It tells us that a relationship exists between concepts in a compound subject. It does *not* tell us what *kind* of relationship this is. In CC, you will recall, *each facet* has its own distinctive facet indicator. In UDC the colon has to act as an 'all purpose' facet indicator to a very large extent.

This is also true of the facet indicators used to introduce the special auxiliaries, - (hyphen) and .0 (point nought). These notational symbols serve to introduce a special auxiliary, but they do not tell us precisely what *kind* of concept is represented by the auxiliary.

In UDC, the colon is also used to express another important set of relationships which exist between concepts and of which no mention has been made so far. These are called *PHASE RELATIONS*.

Again we owe this term to Ranganathan who recognizes five kinds of phase relation. These are:

1 *General phase*
A relationship of a general, or unspecified, nature existing between subjects.

    eg   Title *'The relationship between geography and history'*
           SA   Geography/*General relation*/History

2 *Bias phase*
Here the subject of a document is directed, or biased, towards a particular group of users.

    eg   Title *'Statistics for historians'*
           SA   Statistics/*Bias*/Historians

3 *Comparison phase*
Subjects treated on a comparative basis.

    eg   Title *'The Decimal Classification and the Colon Classification compared'*
           SA   Library science/Classification/Systems/DC/*Compared to*/CC

4 *Difference phase*
The difference between subjects is concentrated upon.

    eg   Title *'The difference between classical and gothic architecture'*
           SA   Architecture/Styles/Classical/*Difference phase*/Gothic

5 *Influencing phase*

The influence of one subject upon another.

 eg Title *'The influence of science on religion'*
   SA Religion/*Influenced by*/Science

When the summarized subject of a document includes a phase relation it is usually called a *COMPLEX SUBJECT.* As such it is distinguished from *compound* and *simple* subjects to which reference has been made. In CC, each of the five kinds of phase relation is allocated its own individual notation.

In UDC we have to rely on the : (colon) to indicate the existence of a phase relationship between concepts. We cannot express the precise kind of phase relation existing.

Consider a document about *'The influence of religion on Renaissance art'.* What kind of subject does this represent?

 Simple – frame 233
 Compound – frame 223
 Complex – frame 237

---

247 (241)

Your answer 911.3:61:(5). No, this is incorrect.

The concept *'Asia'* is provided for by a *common auxiliary* of Place. You are familiar with the use of these common auxiliaries. They are already provided with their individualizing facet indicators and there is no need to use the : (colon) when employing them in the further subdivision of a class.

Please return to frame 241 and select another answer to the question.

Your answer should be 553+622(73).

It must be stated that an extensive use of the + (plus sign) is *neither recommended nor required*.

In the majority of instances were it *could* be employed in the construction of a class number, the documents concerned should be treated as *composite documents*. That is, they should be regarded as dealing with *two or more discrete subjects* and should be provided with two or more *discrete class numbers*.

In this way, the document about *'Economic geology and mining in the USA'* would be allocated *two* class numbers

   553(73)
   622(73)

However, the occurance of *'and'* in a title usually implies a *relationship* between concepts. For example, *'Science and history'* implies a document about the *relationship* between science and history, not that these are treated as two *separate* subjects.

Thus, in most cases, *neither* the + (plus sign) *nor* two class numbers are required, but rather the use of the : (colon) which indicates a relationship between the concepts so linked.

Now please continue with Part II of this section of the course dealing with UDC on frame 249.

SECTION 4: UNIVERSAL DECIMAL CLASSIFICATION/PART II

In our examination of UDC so far we have made no explicit mention of the problem of citation order in compound subjects. In this part of the course we shall pay particular attention to this problem and consider the extent to which general principles of helpful citation order may be applied to UDC.

You have already seen that practical classification with UDC involves a high degree of synthesis. The indexer is required to analyse the subject of a document into its constituent elements and then to recombine, or synthesize, these concepts within the provisions and limitations of the classification scheme.

In the Colon Classification, the process of synthesis in the construction of compound class numbers is placed under strict control. In all main classes, synthesis is determined by the prescribed citation order PME...ST.

Now the situation in UDC is very different. In general, UDC has *no prescribed citation order.*

It follows from this that the indexer is given a very large degree of choice in deciding upon the citation order of concepts in compound subjects.

We say a degree of choice because the indexer is not given *total* freedom regarding citation order. In certain cases the citation order in compound subjects is predetermined.

Obviously, when a compound subject is *enumerated* in the main tables, ie provided with a *ready-made* class number, then the indexer has no choice in determining the citation order within that compound.

Suppose, for example, that you have to classify a document about *'Diseases of the throat'.*

The subject of this document is provided with a *ready-made* class number at *616.22.*

This class number can be analysed as follows:

61	Medicine
616	Disease
616.2	Respiratory disease
616.22	Throat

It can be seen that, in this case, *Part of body* is subordinated to *Disease* and thus the citation order in the compound is:

Medicine/Disease/Respiratory disease/Throat

Because this class number is enumerated, no synthesis, or 'number-building', is required on the part of the indexer. Consequently, the citation order in this compound subject is *predetermined.*

Continue on the next frame

When synthesis is required in the expression of compound subjects, UDC occasionally provides an *indication* of a possible citation order to be followed.

Such an indication is provided by a *directive* in the schedules. Please turn to class 59 Zoology.

At 591.2 you will see an example of such a directive thus:

591.2 Diseases, injuries, malformations etc.

Zoopathology. Teratology

:592/59 Specific animals affected

We can infer from this directive that UDC expects the citation order in class 59 to be,

Zoology/Disease/Specific animal

Following this directive, a document about 'Diseases of the honey-bee' would be assigned the number

591.2:595.799

The citation order in this compound class number is

Zoology/Disease/Honey-bee

(NB: We have omitted any reference to the position of the concept 'specific diseases' in the citation order as this raises a problem not to be dealt with here.)

Such directives, however, do *not* have the status of mandatory instructions. UDC certainly does not forbid other possible citation orders, eg in this case

Zoology/Honey-bee/Disease

595.799:591.2

Consider the document '*A bibliography of physical anthropology*' and its classification by UDC. Which of the following statements is true?

You must assign to this document the class
number 016:572   — frame 266
You may assign to this document the class
number 572:016   — frame 258

251   (260, 264)
Your answer 582.734(Roses):581.24. Yes, you are correct.

As shown in your table, the categories present in the discipline Botany, cited in PME...ST order, are:

$$P_1 \quad P_2 \quad E$$
Botany/Plant/Organ/Processes

If we cite the concepts present in a summarization of the document about *'Fungus diseases of roses'* in this order we get,

$$P_1 \qquad E$$
Botany/Roses/Fungus diseases

This translates into the UDC class number

582.734(Roses):581.24

Note that in this class number it is necessary to employ a *verbal extension* in order to specify the concept 'rose'. The class number 582.734 alone is not specific enough as several plants, including roses, must be classed here.

Continue on frame 261

---

252   (259)
You think that both class numbers are correct. You are right.

The scheme allows for the intercalation of Space concepts and therefore *both* class numbers are permissable in terms of UDC. In classifying this particular document we can choose *either* of the two citation orders exemplified:

1   Education/Higher education/Universities/Germany/19th century
378.4 (430) "18"

2   Education/Germany/Higher education/Universities/19th century
37 (430) 84 "18"

Obviously, once a choice of citation order has been made it must be kept to, otherwise chaos will result.

If, in class 37, the indexer decides to employ citation order 1 above, he must not, at a later date and with another document, use citation order 2.

When a citation order for a given class in a given collection is chosen the alternatives are rejected permanently.

Thus, in any retrieval situation where UDC is the index language used, it is essential for the indexer to determine a citation order formula for each class and to adhere to it in order to maintain consistency.

Continue on the next frame

253   (252)

Although UDC does not *prescribe* a citation order, it does *suggest* a citation order in the introduction to the English Abridged Edition BS1000 A:1961 (page 9, paragraph 5).

The suggested order is stated in terms of:

1   Main table number
2   Special auxiliaries: ' (apostrophe) .0 (point nought) - (hyphen)
3   Common auxiliaries: Viewpoint Place Time Form Language

Now we stress that this is only a *suggested* citation order, you do *not* need to commit it to memory. It is only presented in the introduction as a guide line, not as a rule of the scheme.

This citation order is *broadly* in agreement with one based on categories, such as PME...ST. It does not, however, go far enough in its analysis of concepts.

The surest way to arrive at a helpful and consistent order is to be guided by those *principles* of citation order which have been demonstrated as helpful.

You have already met the citation order PME...ST in the Colon Classification. You are required, for the purposes of this course, to apply this citation order to UDC as far as the scheme will allow.

Continue on the next frame

---

254   (253)

Ranganathan's five Fundamental Categories of concepts, Personality, Matter, Energy, Space and Time are *recognizable* in UDC and can therefore be used as a guide to selecting a helpful citation order in the construction of compound class numbers.

Moreover, by using the formula PME...ST Form as a general guide to the selection of citation order, consistency in classification will be ensured.

Although these categories of concepts are recognizable in UDC, they are in no way made *explicit* within the scheme. Facet analysis in UDC is, at best, inconsistent. It most certainly does not analyse each subject area into clearly defined facets on the basis of PMEST and display them, accordingly, in the schedule.

However, if you are to use PME...ST as a guide to citation order in your practical classification with UDC, you must be able to identify these categories as they manifest themselves in any given subject area in the scheme.

As an aid to this, you are provided with a table showing the categories, and citation order of these categories, in each of the main classes of the 6th edition of the Colon Classification. Space, Time and Form are omitted from this table as they are common to all the main classes. See Appendix.

These classes are arranged in UDC order, beginning with 02 Library science and ending with 93 History.

When classifying a document by UDC, consult this table if you are in doubt as to the nature of the categories present, and their precise citation order, in the subject area within which you are working.

Take, for example, a document belonging to the subject area Library science, *'Book selection in school libraries'*.

Consult your table and decide which of the following UDC class numbers for this document conforms to the citation order of concepts PME...ST.

    025.21:027.8   – frame 264
    027.8:025.21   – frame 260

---

255 (261)

Your answer: Geography/Manitoba/Economic/Atlases. No, this is not correct.

It is *possible* to employ this citation order in classifying the document *'An economic atlas of Manitoba'* by UDC. The resulting class number is
    917.127:33(084.4)

However, the ciation order adopted does *not* conform to PME...ST. You have decided to cite the concept 'Manitoba' first. In other words you imply that Manitoba is a Personality concept in Geography and this is not true.

Please return to frame 261 and reconsider the question, consulting your table which gives you the CC analysis of Geography. Then select another answer to the question.

---

256 (259)

Your answer. Only class number B, ie 37(430)84"18", is correct.

No, you are wrong.

Your answer implies that class number A can be regarded as incorrect and this is not true.

Please return to frame 259 and read again about the choice of citation orders in UDC. Then select the correct answer to the question and continue with the course.

257 (261)

Your answer: Geography/Atlases/Manitoba/Economics. No, you are wrong.

You *could* use this citation order when classifying *'An economic atlas of Manitoba'* by UDC. You would arrive at the following class number:

912(084.4)(712.7):33

This citation order does *not*, however, conform to the order PME...ST. The concept cited first is 'atlases' and this does not constitute a Personality concept in Geography.

Please return to frame 261 and reconsider the question. Look at your table which gives you the CC analysis of Geography and then select another answer to the question.

---

258 (250)

Your answer, you may assign the class number 572:016. Correct.

According to the principles of subject analysis, the document *'A bibliography of physical anthropology'* would be summarized as

Physical anthropology/Bibliography

On translating this analysis into UDC, it is found that the scheme provides no common auxiliary of Form for the concept 'bibliography'. In order to denote this concept the indexer must use the main table numbers 011/016.

In this case the appropriate class is 016 Special subject bibliographies. At 016 there is a directive 'By: . . . ' which tells the indexer to subdivide this class further by appropriate parts of the scheme using the colon. This directive is *not* an instruction and does *not* prevent adherence to the citation order

Physical anthropology/Bibliography

giving the class number 572:016

Continue on the next frame

In the majority of cases, the indexer is granted considerable freedom of choice as to the citation order he adopts in the construction of compound class numbers.

When using the : (colon) to link concepts, the indexer is at liberty to decide in what order the concepts should be cited.

Consider, for example, *'Insect pests: a guide to the pests of houses, gardens, farms and pets'*.

An appropriate UDC class number for this document is,

595.7:591.65

This class number follows the citation order

Zoology/Insects/Economic zoology/Harmful animals

However, UDC equally permits the indexer to assign the class number

591.65:595.7

In this compound class number, the indexer has adopted the citation order

Zoology/Economic zoology/Harmful animals/Insects

In classifying this document, the indexer is free to adopt whichever citation order he considers most helpful. Both the above class numbers are acceptable in terms of UDC.

Another feature of UDC which allows for the flexibility of citation order in the notational plane, is the ability to *intercalate* certain concepts in compound class numbers.

Some of the common auxiliaries are allocated notations in which the facet indicators possess both an *opening* and a *closure* sign. The notations for Place and Time, for example, are

(1/9)

" "

The numerical notations are *enclosed* within ( ), round brackets, and
" ", quotation marks.

When concepts possess this kind of 'packaged' notation, it is possible to insert them in any desired position in a compound class number.

This process is referred to as the *intercalation* of concepts. Intercalation increases the degree of freedom in choosing citation order.

Suppose that you have to classify a document about *'The British Liberal Party'*.

This document can be assigned the class number

329.12 (41-4)

Here you have employed the citation order

Politics/Political parties/Liberals/United Kingdom

It can equally be assigned the class number

329 (41-4) 12

In this case you have employed the citation order

Politics/Political parties/United Kingdom/Liberals

This latter citation order, which is the one exemplified in the schedule at 329, is achieved by *intercalating* the Space concept, United Kingdom, within the compound class number.

Again, both these class numbers, representing different citation orders, are equally acceptable by UDC.

Notice that in the class number 329 (41-4) 12 the decimal point has been dropped. Except when used as a facet indicator in conjunction with 0 (zero), the decimal point in UDC serves only as a separating device employed after three digits. The intercalation of (41-4) after 329 obviates this function.

Suppose you have to classify a document about *'The development of the university in Germany during the nineteenth century'*. You consider two class numbers for this document,

    A   378.4 (430) "18"
    B   37 (430) 84 "18"

Which of the following statements is true?

    Only class number A is correct. – frame 263
    Only class number B is correct. – frame 256
    Both class numbers are correct. – frame 252

---

260 (254)

Your answer 027.8:025.21. Correct.

The citation order within the discipline Library science is:

$$P_1 \qquad M \qquad E$$

Library science/Libraries/Stock/Operations

If we cast the summarization of the document *'Book selection in school libraries'* into the citation order PME...ST, we get, therefore,

$$P_1 \qquad\qquad\qquad E$$

Library science/School libraries/Book selection

The translation of this citation order of concepts into UDC notation gives us the class number

    027.8:025.21

Now try another example, this time from the discipline Botany. Which of the following class numbers for the document *'Fungus diseases of roses'* conforms to the citation order PME...ST?

    582.734(Roses):581.24   – frame 251
    581.24:582.734(Roses)   – frame 265

As was stated earlier, concepts that can be regarded as manifestations of the categories Personality, Matter, Energy, Space and Time are recognizable in UDC even though these categories are by no means made explicit within the schedules of the scheme.

Consequently, if we are to use PME...ST as a guide in deciding upon a generally helpful citation order in compound subjects, considerable emphasis is placed upon subject analysis.

In practical classification with UDC, thorough and consistent work at the stage of the subject analysis of a document is essential.

At this point, the indexer must decide what categories the constituent concepts of the analysis represent and, therefore, in what order they should *preferably* be cited.

It is to help you make these important decisions that you have been provided with the table showing the CC analysis of subject areas into PM and E categories.

The resulting subject analysis at the level of summarization will thus state,

1 The subject area to which this document belongs, ie its *basic class*

2 The phenomena studied cast in PME...ST order. Concepts of Form should appear last in the citation order.

The indexer can then translate this analysis into a UDC class number which follows this desired citation order *so far as the limitations of the scheme allow.*

Consider the document '*An economic atlas of Manitoba*'. The following summarizations of this document employ different citation orders.

Which of these subject analyses is cast in the citation order PME...ST Form?

Geography/Manitoba/Economic/Atlases   – frame 255
Geography/Economic/Manitoba/Atlases   – frame 267
Geography/Atlases/Manitoba/Economics   – frame 257

---

262 (264)
Your decision, 581.24:582.734 (Roses). No, you are repeating the same kind of error.

You are still failing to observe a PME...ST citation order where this is permissible in the construction of a compound class number in UDC.

The class number you chose represents the citation order

Botany/Plant diseases/Fungus diseases/Roses

Look at your table again and you will see that these concepts are *not* cited in the order PME...ST. In the discipline Botany, *plants* constitute the *Personality* concepts, while *Diseases* fall within the Processes or *Energy* facet.

Please return to frame 264. Consider the question carefully, then select the correct answer and continue with the course.

263 (259)

You say that *only* class number A, ie 378.4(430)"18", is correct.

This means that you think class number B is in some way incorrect. This is not true.

Please return to frame 259 and read through the text on the choice of citation order in UDC again. Then select the correct answer and continue with the course.

---

264 (254)

Your answer 025.21:027.8. No, this is not the correct answer.

This is a perfectly acceptable UDC class number but it does *not* conform to the citation order PME...ST.

Remember that you are asked to follow PME...ST wherever a choice of citation order is given.

Look at your table again and you will see that the citation order in the class Library science is

$$P_1 \quad M \quad E$$

Library science/Libraries/Stock/Operations

Consequently, if we cast the subject analysis of the document *'Book selection in school libraries'* in this citation order, we get

$$P_1 \qquad\qquad E$$

Library science/School libraries/Book selection

The translation of this analysis into a UDC class number conforming to the citation order PME...ST gives us, therefore,

027.8:025.21

Now try another example, this time from the discipline Botany. The document is titled *'Fungus diseases of roses'*.

Consult your table showing you the categories present in this discipline, and their citation order, and then decide which of the following UDC class numbers for the above document conforms to the citation order PME...ST.

582.734(Roses):581.24 – frame 251
581.24:582.734(Roses) – frame 262

265 (260)

Your answer, 581.24:582.734(Roses). No, this time you are wrong.

Although this is an acceptable UDC class number for the document concerned, the citation order it represents does *not* conform to PME...ST.

Remember that you are asked to follow PME...ST wherever a *choice* of citation order is given in UDC.

Please return to frame 260 and consider the question once more. Having consulted your table carefully, select the correct answer and proceed with the course.

---

266 (250)

Your answer, you must assign the class number 016.572. Wrong.

According to the principles of subject analysis, the document *'A bibliography of physical anthropology'* would be summarized as

Physical anthropology/Bibliography

On translating this analysis into UDC, it is found that the scheme provides no common auxiliary of Form for the concept 'bibliography' In order that this concept may be denoted the indexer must use the main table numbers 011/016.

In this case the appropriate class is 016 Special subject bibliographies. At 016 there is a directive 'By: . . . ' which tells the indexer to subdivide this class further by appropriate parts of the scheme using the colon eg 016:572.

This directive is *not* an instruction and UDC does *not* prevent adherence to the citation order

Physical anthropology/Bibliography

giving the class number 572:016.

Please continue with the course on frame 259.

Your answer: Geography/Economic/Manitoba/Atlases. Yes, you are right.

If we apply the citation order PME...ST Form to the subject area Geography, we arrive at the above order in the summarization of this document.

Economic geography constitutes the Personality concept and this is followed by Space and Form, thus,

P   S   Form

Geography/Economic/Manitoba/Atlases

The translation of this analysis, employing the desired citation order, gives us the class number

911.3:33(712.7)(084.4)

It should be stated that our use of PME...ST Form is not an attempt to *force* the Colon Classification upon UDC. We are only employing this principle of order, which is applicable to all subject areas, as a guide in deciding upon a helpful citation order in compound subjects when such a choice is allowed.

It might be helpful to recapitulate briefly upon what has been said about citation orders in UDC and the way in which you are required to apply the scheme for the purposes of this course.

You should then attempt some examples of practical classification for yourself.

SUMMARY

1 UDC has no *prescribed* citation order.
2 In the majority of cases, it is the responsibility of the indexer to decide upon the citation order to be employed in compound subjects.
3 In such a situation, it is essential to decide upon a citation order formula for each class *and to adhere strictly to it.*
4 The surest way to arrive at such a decision is to be guided by principles of helpful citation order.
5 One such principle is the citation order based upon the categories PMEST. This is applicable to all subject areas.
6 You are required to follow the citation order PME...ST Form *whenever a choice of citation order is given.*

Continue on the next frame

It would be useful for you to classify the following examples by UDC before going on to the next section of the course.

For each document produce:

a) a subject analysis, at the level of summarization, cast in the citation order PME...ST form.

b) a UDC class number which employs this citation order as far as the scheme will allow.

Remember the tables in the Appendix which may help in your analyses and then check your answers against those suggested on frame 349.

1 Library resources in the Greater London area: No 5 Agricultural libraries.

2 Therapy through hypnosis.

3 Cereal diseases: Ministry of Agriculture, Fisheries and Food Bulletin No 129.

4 Roots of contemporary American architecture: a series of essays.

5 The selected poems of Robert Graves.

Continue on frame 349.

SUBJECT CATALOGUING: A FOREWORD

We must now return to the consideration of indexes and here we shall re-capitulate, and expand, upon some of the points already made in Section 1. You may therefore find it useful to refer back to the introductory section of the course.

This present brief section is to be read as preliminary to a more detailed examination of some of the techniques of index construction which will follow.

You will recall that a *library catalogue* constitutes a complete record of the library's collection of documents. From now on we shall refer to them simply as *catalogues*.

Bibliographies are distinguished from catalogues in that the documents they record are not necessarily held in a particular library. The limitations placed upon the documents included in a bibliography are those such as place of publication, date of publication or subject content.

An *index*, in the context of information retrieval, is some kind of physical mechanism, or tool, which serves to indicate to the searcher those parts of an information store which are potentially relevant to a request.

Catalogues and bibliographies are both forms of indexes. They are similar in function and in structure. For the purposes of our practical subject indexing we shall concentrate on, and refer primarily to, the construction of catalogues.

In the process of information retrieval catalogues help to overcome the limitations of the shelf arrangement of documents, itself a form of index. They do this primarily by providing *multiple access* to documents via the medium of document *substitutes* or *representations*.

Catalogues are found in a variety of *physical forms*, for example, *printed book catalogues, microforms* and *card catalogues*. You can find descriptions of these types of catalogue in other textbooks and we need not pursue them in any detail here.

The essential functions of a catalogue, and the principles upon which it is constructed, are not affected by its physical form. In this course we are concerned with the *principles* of catalogue construction and therefore physical form is of little direct interest. Nevertheless, it is important to envisage the appearance of a catalogue and for this reason we shall refer, almost exclusively, to the widely adopted card catalogue in our consideration of catalogue construction.

(NB: The method of indexing called *post-coordinate indexing* gives rise to physical forms of indexes which differ from the more 'traditional' catalogues mentioned above. These, and the principles upon which they are constructed, are to be considered later.)

In a card catalogue, each document substitute is in the form of an *index card* or *catalogue card* usually of a standard size 5 X 3 inches.

We have already seen that theoretically a document can have any number of such substitutes or representations in the catalogue. Each document substitute constitutes an *entry* in the catalogue for that document. Practical considerations do, in fact, limit the number of entries that it is feasible to make for any given document.

Now each entry indicates the inclusion of the document within a particular class of documents. These classes are defined by such characteristics as *authorship* or *subject content.*

Since it is possible to have a number of entries for a single document we are able to display that document in a number of classes to which it belongs. Thus we provide for *multiple access* to the document. That is access via the different characteristics which it possesses and which might be helpful for the purposes of its retrieval.

Each entry made for a document contains a statement of a class of which the document forms a part. These statements form the *heading* of the entry (written at the top or 'head' of say a catalogue card) and entries are arranged or filed according to their headings which may be either verbal or notational statements.

Those entries which show the inclusion of documents in classes defined by authorship are called *author entries*, in classes defined by subject content, *subject entries.*

If an entry acts as a substitute or representation of a document it must contain a *description* of that document in order to individualize it. These document descriptions include such elements as the document's author, its title, publisher, place and date of publication, pagination etc.

In order that we can retrieve the document itself, each entry must also state *precisely* where in the library that document is stored or shelved. This locational element is sometimes referred to as the *call mark* or *call number* of the document.

The call number of a document is *not* synonymous with its *class number.* When a library arranges its documents in classified order, the class number of a document is obviously an important element in its call number. The call number may well include other elements, however, such as a *collection number* indicating the particular collection in which the document is housed, eg reference collection.

Not *all* library collections are arranged in classified order. In these cases a document will possess no class number but it must still be provided with a call number for locational purposes. Sometimes accession order is used as an alternative to classified order in the shelf arrangement of documents. In such a situation the accession number of a document will act as its call number and indicate its precise shelf location.

So far we have established that the library catalogue, as an index to the library's collection, contains entries which play the role of document substitutes displaying the inclusion of documents in classes defined by different characteristics. These classes are stated in the headings on the document entries. In response to requests for information we search those classes of documents, ie limited parts of the total store, which are *potentially relevant* to the request. Having located a potentially relevant class, the catalogue will reveal the individual documents contained in that class and will tell the searcher just where these documents can be found within the library.

In addition to entries for individual documents, catalogues also contain directions which *refer* the searcher from one heading to another heading under which potentially relevant information, in the form of document entries, can be located. These are called *references* in the catalogue and thus we have *author references, title references, subject references* etc, depending on the type of heading referred to and from.

The assigning of author and title headings for entries and references in catalogues is commonly termed *author/title cataloguing* or *author/title indexing*. It is not the particular concern of this course. Sets of rules have been formulated to guide the cataloguer in author/title cataloguing and to help ensure standardization of practice. Such a *code of cataloguing rules* is the *Anglo-American cataloguing rules* (2nd edn, 1978).

The *description* of documents in catalogue entries is called *descriptive cataloguing* and this also falls outside our present interest. Again, rules have been formulated to ensure standardization of practice in descriptive cataloguing and these are contained in such codes as AACR.

This course is devoted to *practical subject indexing* and thus our prime concern is with the construction of headings and references which facilitate the retrieval of documents, through the medium of indexes, in response to requests for information on *named subjects*. The assigning of such headings and references for incorporation into library catalogues is usually called *subject cataloguing*.

Subject cataloguing forms an integral part of the total cataloguing process and any distinction between this and other aspects of cataloguing must be somewhat artificial. However, given the limitations of this programmed course, it is necessary for us to concentrate, almost exclusively, on the problems of subject cataloguing. From this viewpoint we shall examine the construction of two types of catalogue or index—the classified catalogue and the alphabetical subject catalogue.

In both cases we shall consider the application of the techniques of chain procedure to the construction of these catalogues. Chain procedure is most certainly not the only method available for subject catalogue construction. However, it does provide a very useful approach to examining basic principles in the construction of subject catalogues, and for this reason it is used in this course. An appreciation of chain procedure is a valuable background to the understanding of other methods, eg PRECIS and the use of lists of subject headings, consideration of which lies outside the scope of this particular volume.

Continue on the next frame

SECTION 5: THE CLASSIFIED CATALOGUE/PART I

The classified catalogue consists traditionally of three separate parts,
namely
1 The classified file.
2 The alphabetical subject index to the classified file.
3 The author index.

In this section of the course our attention will be focused principally
on the alphabetical subject index to the classified file and the techniques
employed in its construction. We shall be particularly concerned with
the method of index construction called *chain indexing*.

Before we proceed to examine chain indexing in any detail, we shall
briefly describe the three parts of the classified catalogue. Each of these
has its own particular functions and all are closely interrelated. Although
we must concentrate on only one aspect of the construction of the
classified catalogue, it is important to bear in mind the total structure of
this kind of index.

Continue on the next frame

---

271 (270)
The AUTHOR INDEX

The author index, or 'author/title index', of a classified catalogue consists
of entries and references arranged in alphabetical order of author and,
where required, title, translator, series etc, headings.

In the conventional card catalogue it will thus consist of a single
alphabetical sequence of 5 X 3 inch cards.

This index therefore allows for the retrieval of documents via known
authors, titles, translators, series etc. It caters for what is commonly
termed the *'author approach'* to information retrieval.

Once the searcher has located the relevant entry in the author index,
the document can be retrieved from its position in a classified shelf
arrangement by means of the call mark included in the entry for that
document.

The problems which arise in making entries and references for the
author index, ie the problems of *'author/title cataloguing'*, lie outside
the scope of this present course.

Continue on the next frame

The CLASSIFIED FILE

The classified file and its alphabetical subject index provide for what is commonly termed the *'subject approach'* to information retrieval. It is these two parts of the classified catalogue that are therefore our prime concern.

Entries made for documents in the classified file are arranged in a *classified order of subjects.* This classified order is determined by the scheme used for the classification of the documents. In this course we shall consider classified catalogues in which UDC is the scheme employed.

You have already had practice in classifying documents by UDC. In the construction of a classified catalogue the class number you assign to a document forms the *heading* for that document's entry in the classified file. Consequently the class number will determine the precise location of that entry in the overall classified arrangement of subjects.

Entries in the classified file are thus arranged, or filed, according to the notation of the classification scheme in use.

The UDC notation uses, in part, arabic numerals and these possess an *ordinal value.* With such symbols we thus have a ready-made *filing order,* 534 files before 535, 535.3 files before 535.4 and so on.

The notation, however, also employs symbols which normally have *no* ordinal value, such as + (plus sign), : (colon), / (oblique stroke) and - (hyphen).

When such symbols are used in a class number a decision must be made as to whether, for example, 534/535 files before or after 534 + 535. In other words, these symbols, / + ( ) etc, are *assigned* an ordinal value within the filing order of the elements in the notation.

On page 10, paragraph 6, of the scheme you can find a statement of the UDC filing order exemplified by class 675 Leather industry.

It is not necessary for you to commit this filing order to memory as you will not be required to employ it. You will not be required to *file* catalogue entries for documents classified by UDC as part of this course. Nor will you be required to arrange such documents on the shelves of a library.

The filing order of the notation is designed to maintain the desired order of *subjects* both on the shelves (ie the documents themselves) and in the classified file (ie the entries for those documents). You will remember that a notation *only maintains an already preferred order*, it does not *determine* it. This order is based on conceptual relations.

In our examination of the structure of the classified catalogue the *citation order* of concepts in a compound class number is of much greater significance than the filing order of the notation. This will become more evident as we proceed.

At this stage it is sufficient for you to bear in mind that, within any given class, the order of entries in a classified file is determined by

1 The *citation order* of concepts in the heading for a compound subject (ie in a compound class number)

2 The *filing order* between such headings

The order of entries in a classified file is not simply a duplicate of the order of documents on the shelves.

To begin with the classified file presents a *single* classified sequence whereas shelf order is often broken into *several* classified sequences by such factors as the physical form of documents, eg one sequence for books, another for pamphlets etc.

Moreover, it is possible for a document to have *more than one entry* in the classified file whereas it can only have one physical location on the shelves.

Initially, however, we shall consider the classified catalogue which, *as a general rule*, contains only one entry for each document in the classified file. *This is called a single entry system.*

This single entry is filed under the class number which denotes the *specific summarization* of the subject content of that document. It is a *specific subject entry*.

The classified file is thus a classified arrangement of subjects contained within documents possessed by the library. It is not a simple repetition of shelf order in the form of document substitutes.

The prime aim of the classified file is to facilitate the retrieval of information about *named subjects*, not the retrieval of named documents.

It achieves this aim principally through the *juxtaposition* of related subjects in a *classified order*.

Continue on the next frame

---

273 (272)

The ALPHABETICAL SUBJECT INDEX

In order to discover what information the library possesses about a particular subject, we must first locate that subject within the classified file. The entries under this subject will describe individual documents and tell us precisely where they can be found upon the shelves.

We have seen, however, that the entries in the classified file are arranged by the notation of the classification scheme. That is, they are arranged in an order that users cannot be expected to be familiar with. Thus entries about, say, town planning are *not* filed under the term 'town planning'. They are filed under the notation for this subject, 711.4.

Obviously all requests for information about subjects are couched, initially, in *natural language*, ie in *words* which *name* those subjects. A library user requests information about 'town planning' not about '711.4'. Nor does he know that 711.4 is the notational expression of this subject and that, therefore, relevant information will be filed under this class number in the classified file.

Thus, to locate a particular subject within the classified file, the statement of that subject in verbal terms must be *translated* into the statement of that subject in notational terms. The *name* of the subject must be translated into its *class number* which determines its location in the classified sequence of subjects.

The first function of the alphabetical subject index to the classified file is to provide for the approach to subjects via their names. Subjects are stated in verbal terms and provided with their corresponding class numbers. By translating the names of subjects into their notations, the alphabetical subject index serves as a key to the locations of subjects within the classified file.

The entries made in the alphabetical subject index do *not* refer to individual documents.

They contain only the names of *subjects* and their corresponding notations.

These entries are then filed in *alphabetical order* of subject names.

Let us consider our example of the subject *town planning*. An entry in the alphabetical subject index for this subject will consist solely of the name of the subject and its class number, thus

Town planning   711.4

This entry will file in the alphabetical subject index as illustrated in the following diagram.

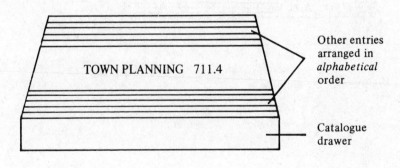

TOWN PLANNING   711.4

Other entries
arranged in
alphabetical
order

Catalogue
drawer

When a catalogue user wants to discover what documents the library contains about town planning, he first consults the *alphabetical subject index* under this *subject*. This tells him that the class number for town planning is 711.4.

He then consults the *classified file* at 711.4. Here he will find entries for the individual *documents* about town planning which have been assigned the class number 711.4 and filed under this heading.

Suppose, for example, that the library possesses the book by Thomas Sharp entitled *'Town planning'*. The entry for this particular document will be filed in the classified file as illustrated below. Guide cards help to break up the classified sequence and direct the user to the required class as indicated.

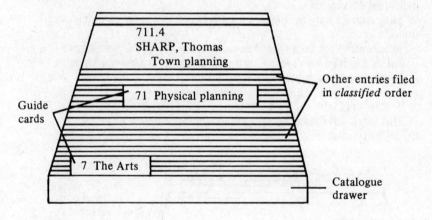

Guide cards

711.4
SHARP, Thomas
Town planning

71 Physical planning

7 The Arts

Other entries filed in *classified* order

Catalogue drawer

Continue on the next frame

From this point on in the course we shall be principally concerned with
the making of entries for subjects in the alphabetical subject index to
the classified file.

At this stage it might therefore be useful to summarize what has been
said so far about the classified catalogue as a whole.

SUMMARY

1 The classified catalogue consists traditionally of three separate parts,
   i The author index
   ii The classified file
   iii The alphabetical subject index to the classified file

2 The classified file and the alphabetical subject index together facilitate
the retrieval of information about named subjects. As such they are our
chief concern in this course.

3 The classified file consists of entries for documents arranged in a classified sequence according to the notation of the classification scheme in use.

4 Before discovering what documents the library possesses about a
particular subject we must therefore know the class number for that
subject.

5 The alphabetical subject index provides this information. It consists
of entries, arranged in alphabetical order, stating the names of subjects
and giving their corresponding class numbers.

6 In the search for information about a named subject the user
   i consults the alphabetical subject index under the verbal statement
     of that subject and is informed of its class number.
   ii consults the classified file under this class number and finds there
     entries for documents about the desired subject.
   iii each of these entries in the classified file will describe an individual
     document and tells the user precisely where in the library it is
     shelved.

Continue on the next frame

CHAIN INDEXING

So far we have established that the first function of the alphabetical subject index is to act as a key to the location of subjects in the classified file. It does this by translating the names of subjects into their corresponding notational expressions or class numbers.

The alphabetical index to the schedules of a classification scheme performs a similar function. It acts as a key to the location of subjects in the schedules, as you know from your practical classification.

Why bother, then, to create an alphabetical index to the classified file when you already have a printed alphabetical index to the schedules of the classification scheme?

The answer lies in the fact that the subjects within the classified file are the subjects of actual documents in a particular collection. Thus the alphabetical index to the classified file is an index to the subjects held in this collection. The purpose of the classified file and its index is to facilitate the retrieval of these documents in response to requests for information on named subjects.

The alphabetical index to the schedules of a classification scheme, however, is an index to *all* the subjects listed in the schedules. It is not an index to the subjects of particular documents.

An attempt to use the alphabetical index to the schedules as an index to the classified file would be unhelpful for two reasons.

1 Many of the subjects listed in the alphabetical index to the schedules would not be represented in the collection of documents and therefore would not be in the classified file.

In such cases consultation of the classified files would be pointless and frustrating to the user.

2 Many of the compound subjects of the documents in the collection, represented by compound class numbers in the classified file, would not be catered for in the alphabetical subject index to the schedules.

In such cases the user would be unable to gain immediate access to the *specific* subject of his search.

It is thus essential for the indexer to create an alphabetical subject index to the classified file. He does this by making the required alphabetical subject index entries as he classifies each document added to the collection.

Continue on the next frame

The subjects named in the alphabetical (from now on shortened to A/Z) subject index to the classified file are the subjects of documents.

As you are aware, the subjects of most documents are *compound subjects*. Compound subjects contain two or more elements. They therefore contains two or more *terms* in their names.

For example, the subject *'Geomorphology of glacial landforms in Scotland'* contains four terms,

geomorphology : landforms : glacial : Scotland

Now there is no one correct or accepted way of naming such a subject as this. These four terms might occur in *any order* in a verbal statement of this subject. Consequently, the catalogue user searching for information about this subject might formulate his request in any one of the possible permutations of these four terms.

He might consult the A/Z index under *any one* of the four terms and reasonably expect to be lead to the specific subject of his search in the classified file.

The problem posed in the naming of most compound subjects for retrieval purposes is that the searcher may begin his search by any one of several terms constituting the verbal statement of that subject.

Thus the A/Z subject index must provide entries that cater for these different approaches to the subject. It must at least provide entries in which each of these terms form the *lead term*. The lead term is the term under which the entry files and by which it is therefore sought. Moreover these entries must ultimately direct the searcher to his desired specific subject in the classified file.

In the case of most compound subjects the provision of entries for all the *permutations* of their constituent terms would result in a quite impossible number of entries in the A/Z subject index.

There are several alternatives to permutation. One very economic and systematic method is known as *CHAIN INDEXING*.

It is to this method that we now turn our attention.

Continue on the next frame

The procedures of chain indexing are based upon the class assigned to a document.

The class number is a notational statement of the subject of the document. It defines the location of this subject within the classified files and therefore the location of entries for documents written *about* this subject.

Remember that we are concerned with a classified catalogue employing a *single entry system*. That is, as a general rule, each document is assigned only *one* class number which represents a *specific summarization* of the subject of the document. This class number provides the heading for the *single specific subject entry* for the document in the classified file.

The structure of every class can be analysed into a 'chain' of concepts.

Take for example a document titled *'The Conservative case'*.

> Subject analysis Politics/Political parties/UK/Conservative
> Class number   329 (41-4) 11

The chain of this class can be written down as follows:

3	Social sciences
32	Political science.
329	Political parties.
(4)	Europe
(41-4)	United Kingdom (of GB and N Ireland)
11	Conservative party

The analysis of a class into its chain is done by consulting the schedules of the classification scheme and writing down *each step of division* within that class, as exemplified above.

Each chain thus reflects the successive application of the *characteristics of division* in a given citation order.

Concepts in chain order are therefore in an order of *successive subordination*.

Chain indexing is so-called because, by this method, the *lead term* in each alphabetical index entry for a given subject is systematically chosen from the *chain* of concepts present in the class assigned to that subject.

Continue on the next frame

278 (277)

Now let us look at the construction of index entries for a particular subject by chain indexing procedure.

With any given class number, the *first* alphabetical index entry made for that subject commences, or *leads* with the last term in the chain and qualifies this with the minimum number of superordinate terms that are necessary to indicate *its precise context*.

Take our example *'The Conservative case'*.

Class no	329 (41-4) 11	
Chain	3	Social sciences
	32	Political science.
	329	Political parties.
	(4)	Europe
	(41-4)	United Kingdom (of GB and N Ireland)
	11	Conservative party

The first alphabetical subject index entry made for the subject of this document is,

Conservative party : United Kingdom 329 (41-4) 11

We have constructed this index entry by taking the term for the *last* concept in the chain, Conservative party, as the *lead* term. In this case it is probably only necessary to qualify this term by the subordinate term, United Kingdom, in order to place it in its precise context.

Suppose the searcher, looking for information upon the subject of this document, consults the alphabetical subject index under this entry.
Which of the following statements will then be true?

He will be lead *directly* to the location of the
specific subject of his search in the classified file. — frame 284
He will *not* be lead *directly* to the location of the
specific subject of his search in the classified file. — frame 287

---

279 (285)

You say that this A/Z index entry will direct him *at once* to the specific subject he is looking for. No. You must consider the problem more carefully.

We have already established that the index entry

Conservative party : United Kingdom : 329(41-4)11

directs the searcher *at once* to the location of his specific subject.

In this instance, however, although our searcher is looking for information about the same subject, he has not consulted this A/Z subject index entry. To all intents and purposes he is unaware of its existence. He has approached his subject under the perfectly acceptable and predictable term *'Political parties'* and has found an A/Z index entry under this term.

Please turn to frame 285. Look carefully at the *exact* form of the A/Z subject index entries made. Then select the correct answer to the question and proceed with the course.

280 (281)

You think that concepts distributed in the classified file are also distributed in the A/Z subject index. This is not so.

You think that the concept Poetry, for example, which constitutes a distributed relative in the classified file, by virtue of the citation adopted in the classification of documents, is also distributed throughout the A/Z subject index.

Please return to frame 281 and look at the two specific A/Z index entries for class numbers 820-1 and 840-1. Remember that those entries file in *alphabetical order*.

Then reconsider the question carefully and proceed with the course.

---

281 (283)

You say that the concepts appear in a reverse order of the citation order employed in the class number. Correct.

In the verbal subject statement of the A/Z index entry

Conservative party : United Kingdom   329(41-4)11

the concept Conservative party is cited *before* United Kingdom. In the class number for the subject it is cited *after* United Kingdom.

By qualifying lead terms, when necessary, by *superordinate* terms from the chain, we are *reversing* the citation order employed in the class number being indexed.

Why bother to reverse the citation order, why not employ the same citation order as the class number?

Let us consider two fairly straightforward subjects this time from class 8, Literature.

1 *'English poetry'*
   Class number 820-1
   Chain   8   Literature
                 820   English literature
                 -1   Poetry

2 *'French poetry'*
   Class number 840-1
   Chain   8   Literature
                 840   French literature
                 -1   Poetry

The two specific A/Z subject index entries for these subjects are,

Poetry : English literature 820-1
Poetry : French literature 840-1

These two entries will file in close proximity in the alphabetical sequence.

Now, by virtue of the citation order adopted in class 8, 'poetry' constitutes a distributed relative in the classified file. It is distributed under the various languages, English, French etc, which appear earlier in the citation order.

Look at the two examples above and then decide which of the following statements you think is true.

Concepts distributed in the classified file are
gathered together in the A/Z subject index.   — frame 288
Concepts distributed in the classified file are
also distributed in the A/Z subject index   — frame 280

---

282 (285)

Your answer: This A/Z index entry will not direct him *at once* to the specific subject he is looking for. Correct.

Only the *specific* A/Z subject index entry provides direct access to the *full class number* for the subject, in this instance 329(41-4)11.

If the user happens to formulate his request at a more general, less specific level he will consult the A/Z subject index under an entry made for one of the superordinate terms in the chain.

eg   Political parties   329
or   United Kingdom : Political parties   329 (41-4)

In such cases he is directed *only part of the way* to the location of the specific class he really wants.

Nevertheless, providing that he has consulted the A/Z index under *any one of the terms in the chain*, he is at least directed to a relevant part of the classified file near to the location of the subject of his search.

Admittedly, this relevant part of the classified file may not be the specific class he wants. For instance, if he looks under *Political parties* he will be directed to 329, if under *UnitedK ingdom :Political parties* to 329(41-4). In fact he needs to arrive at class 329(41-4)11 before his request is satisfied.

However, on arriving at one of these less specific classes, the classified order of entries in the classified file will lead him successfully to the specific class he desires, ie to class 329(41-4)11. The provision of *'guide'* or *'feature'* cards, displaying class numbers and their verbal translations, break up the classified sequence into manageable proportions and help in the process of guiding.

Thus, at whatever 'level' of the chain of concepts the user chooses to consult the A/Z subject index, on entering the classified file the classified order of subjects will guide him to the specific subject of his search.

We can see, then, that the series of entries produced by chain indexing procedure allows the user to gain access to the desired specific subject in the classified file by consulting the A/Z subject index under any one of that subject's constituent terms.

Continue on the next frame

So the order of subjects in the classified file and the order of subjects in the A/Z subject index are *complementary*. Let us look at the relationship between these two orders a little more closely.

We said that concepts in *chain order* are in an order of *successive subordination*. Take the chain of concepts in the subject represented by our class number 329(41-4)11 once more.

3	Social sciences
32	Political science.
329	Political parties.
(4)	Europe
(41-4)	United Kingdom (of GB and N Ireland)
11	Conservative party

When we analyse a class number into its chain, as above, we reveal the *citation order* of concepts employed in that class number.

As you already know, concepts which appear after the first cited concept constitute *distributed relatives*.

Distributed relatives are scattered to varying degrees in the classified file.

Their position within any given class, and therefore the degree of scatter to which they are subjected, is determined by their position in the citation order of concepts within that class.

In class 32, for instance, individual political parties, eg Conservatives, will be subjected to a greater degree of scatter than individual countries, eg United Kingdom. Individual political parties appear later in the citation order, and 'lower' in the chain order of a class number, than do individual countries.

We said that, when the lead term in an A/Z subject index entry requires qualification in order to indicate its precise context, this qualification is provided by the minimum number of appropriate superordinate terms from the chain.

eg   Conservative party : United Kingdom 329(41-4)11

In an A/Z subject index entry such as this, in which order are the concepts cited in the verbal statement of the subject?

In the same order as the citation order
employed in the class number   – frame 286
In a reverse order of the citation order
employed in the class number   – frame 281

284 (278)

You say that the searcher will be lead *directly* to the location of the specific subject of his search in the classified file. Correct.

The index entry consulted is

Conservative party : United Kingdom 329 (41-4) 11

The searcher is looking for information about the Conservative party in the United Kingdom and this A/Z subject index entry directs him to class number 329(41-4)11 in the classified file.

Here he will find filed entries for documents about this subject. He will find entries for documents about the *specific subject* of his search eg '*The Conservative case*'.

Thus the first A/Z index entry made for a subject gives the searcher *direct* access to the full class number for that subject.

It is called the *specific A/Z subject index entry*.

The specific A/Z subject index entry for class 329(41-4)11 is

Conservative party : United Kingdom 329(41-4)11

Continue on the next frame

---

285 (284)

In providing the specific A/Z subject index entry we have by no means provided for *every* possible approach to the specific subject.

The person searching for information about the Conservative party in the United Kingdom might well begin by consulting the A/Z subject index under such terms as *United Kingdom, Politics* or *Political parties*.

Requests for information about a subject are often formulated in more general terms than the statement of the specific subject. The user may approach his subject at a number of different *levels* and by a number of different *terms*.

So far we have only provided for the user who happens to consult the A/Z subject index under the term *Conservative*.

Consequently, every appropriate term in the chain is indexed as a *lead term* qualified by such superordinate terms as are necessary to set it in its context. This is to make sure that, no matter what level the searcher begins at, the term appropriate to that level can be located in the A/Z subject index.

Each lead term is indexed to the class number appropriate to its level in the conceptual chain.

Take again our subject represented by the class number 329(41-4)11 analysed in the chain

3	Social sciences
32	Political science.
329	Political parties.
(4)	Europe
(41-4)	United Kingdom (of GB and N Ireland)
11	Conservative party

The specific A/Z subject index entry is
Conservative party : United Kingdom   329(41-4)11
The procedure of chain indexing would generate *at least* the subsequent index entries:

United Kingdom : Political parties   329(41-4)
Europe : Political parties   329(4)
Political parties   329
Political science   32
Social sciences   3

Other problems raised by this example will be dealt with as you proceed with the course and refine the procedures of chain indexing.

Suppose the searcher looking for information about the Conservative party in the United Kingdom consults the A/Z subject index under the term *Political parties.*

Which of the following statements is true?

This A/Z index entry will direct him *at once* to
the specific subject he is looking for   – frame 279
This A/Z index entry will not direct him *at once*
to the specific subject he is looking for   – frame 282

---

286   (283)
You think that the concepts in the verbal subject statement are cited in the *same order* as in the class number for this subject.

No, this is not true.

Return to frame 283 and look at the analysis of class number 329(41-4)11 carefully. Surely the concept Conservative party appears *last* in the citation order of this class number.

Examine the A/Z subject index entry in question and the citation order employed in the *verbal statement* of the subject in this entry.

Then select the correct answer and proceed with the course.

287 (278)

You think that the searcher will not be lead *directly* to the location of the specific subject of his search in the classified file. No, you are wrong.

Remember that our hypothetical searcher is looking for information about the specific subject *Conservative party in the United Kingdom* and that entries for documents about this particular subject are located in the classified file under the class number 329(41-4)11.

Before his search can be successfully concluded he must arrive at this point in the classified order of subjects. To this end he must first consult the A/Z subject index in order to translate a verbal statement of his subject into a class number.

Now please return to frame 278. Look carefully at the class number for the document, its chain and the construction and form of the A/Z subject index entry in question.

Then select the correct answer to the question and continue with the course.

---

288 (281)

You think that concepts distributed in the classified file are gathered together in the A/Z subject index. You are right.

The concept 'poetry', for example, is distributed in the classified file. Nevertheless, the searcher is able to go to the *single location* within the A/Z subject index, ie he can consult this index under the term 'poetry', and find there entries which serve as a key to the several locations of this concept in the classified file.

eg   Poetry : English literature   820-1
      Poetry : French literature   840-1

By *reversing* citation order and then arranging the resulting verbal subject statements in alphabetical order, the A/Z subject index collects together those concepts which have been scattered in the classified file by virtue of the citation order employed in classifying.

Thus, in addition to serving as a key to the location of subjects in the classified file the A/Z subject index has as its second major function the *collocation of distributed relatives*.

If concepts in the A/Z subject index entries were listed in the *same citation order* employed in the classification of these subjects the result would be much less helpful. The index would then simply *repeat* an order already present in the classified file, it would not *complement* it.

The repetition of the citation order of the class number would result in A/Z subject index entries such as the following:

Literature	8
Literature:English	820
Literature:English:Poetry	820-1
Literature:French	840
Literature:French:Poetry	840-1

In addition to simply repeating an order to be found in the classified file, all these entries would file under the *same* term 'Literature'.

We should *not* have provided for access to subjects by each of their constituent terms and there would be *no* collocation of distributed relatives.

Continue on the next frame

---

289 (288)

Before examining the practical procedures of chain indexing in more detail in the second part of this section, we shall briefly summarize the main points made so far concerning this method.

SUMMARY

1 Chain indexing provides a systematic and economic method of selecting A/Z subject index entries for compound subjects.

2 The index entries made for a given subject are based upon the *chain* of concepts present in the class assigned to that subject.

3 The *specific A/Z subject index entry* is constructed by *leading* with the last term in the chain and qualifying this by the minimum number of superordinate terms required to indicate its precise context.

The specific A/Z subject index entry directs the searcher to the *full class number* for the subject.

4 Index entries are then made for *each* of the other terms in the chain that are liable to be *sought* by the user looking for information about the specific subject.

In each entry the lead term is qualified by the minimum number of superordinate terms and indexed to the class number appropriate to its level in the chain.

5 The series of A/Z index entries so produced allows the searcher to gain access to the location of the specific subjects in the classified file via *any one* of the potentially sought terms in the chain.

If he consults the specific index entry he is lead *directly* to the specific subject in the classified file.

If he consults one of the other entries he is lead to a part of the classified file near to the subject of his search and the classified order of subjects then guides him to the specific subject.

6 By chain indexing procedure, the verbal subject statement in each A/Z index entry *reverses* the citation order employed in the class number for that subject. The A/Z subject index thus provides an order of subjects which *complements* that in the classified file and effects the *collocation of distributed relatives*.

The following is an illustration of chain indexing applied to our fairly straightforward example of the document about *'English poetry'*.

Title	*'English poetry'*	
SA	Literature/English/Poetry	
Class number	820-1	
Chain	8	Literature
	820	English literature
	-1	Poetry

A/Z subject index entries

Poetry : English literature	820-1
English literature	820
Literature	8

Now proceed with the second part of this section on the next frame.

SECTION 5: THE CLASSIFIED CATALOGUE/PART II

So far we have looked at the structure of the classified catalogue with
particular reference to the structure of the A/Z subject index as the key
to the location of subjects in the classified file. We have also considered
the basic principles of chain indexing, an economic and systematic
method of selecting entries for the A/Z subject index.

We shall now go on to examine in more detail the practical procedures
involved in making A/Z subject index entries by the chain indexing
method for the subjects of particular documents.

As you read through the subsequent pages you should always bear
in mind that an A/Z subject index entry is only made if it helps the
user locate the desired subject in the classified file.

The procedures of chain indexing which we shall now describe help
to ensure that the resulting index entries fulfil this criterion.
Continue on the next frame

---

291 (290)

Having classified a document, the first stage in chain indexing is to analyse
the class assigned to that document in order to reveal its *conceptual chain,*
ie the chain of concepts which go to form the subject of the document.

This analysis must always be carried out by consulting the *schedules* of
the classification scheme.

We are analysing a *subject* not a class number. We must state *every step
of division* in that subject and we can by no means rely on the class number
itself to reveal these steps.

Moreover, each step of division should be stated, as far as possible, by a
single word.

eg	Subject	'Secondary schools'	
	Class no	373.5	
	Chain	3	Social sciences
		37	Education
		373	Secondary
		373.5	Schools

These points will be further developed as you proceed with the course.

Suppose you have classified, by UDC, the document *'Select methods of
metallurgical assaying'*, class number 669.9.

The first step in the chain of this class is,

    6 Technology

Now write down the complete analysis of the conceptual chain of this
class by consulting the UDC schedules and stating each step of division by
a single word. Then turn to frame 299.

292 (299)

Your answer:

      Assaying : Metallurgy   669.9

Quite right.

    The specific index entry for 669.9 leads with the last term in the chain, 'assaying'. In this case the use of the superordinate term 'metallurgy' as the only qualifier is quite sufficient to indicate the precise subject context.

    This verbal statement of the specific subject is indexed to the full class number 669.9.

    We might note here that the qualification of lead terms by all the superordinate terms in the chain is in most cases unnecessary. While the resulting A/Z entries are not 'wrong', they tend to be clumsy. For example in the index entry

        Assaying : Metallurgy : Chemical technology   669.9

the terms 'chemical technology' add nothing of real value to the verbal statement of the specific subject 'assaying:metallurgy'. They are redundant in this particular subject context.

Continue on the next frame

---

293 (292, 296)

Having made the specific A/Z index entry, we must now make an index entry for every other term in the chain which is liable to be sought by a user looking for information about this subject.

    In other words, we must ensure that every *sought term* in the chain forms the *lead term* in an A/Z subject index entry.

    In each index entry the lead term is only qualified by superordinate terms if these are required to indicate its precise context. Qualification is always provided by the *minimum number* of necessary superordinate terms.

    In each index entry the lead term is indexed to the class number appropriate to its level in the chain, ie to the class number which represents that particular verbal subject statement.

    Here is the chain of class 669.9 once more.

6	Technology
66	Chemical
669	Metallurgy
669.9	Assaying

    The first A/Z subject index made by chain procedure was the specific subject entry

        Assaying : Metallurgy   669.9

Now we move up the chain providing index entries for each of the potentially sought terms.

    Which of the following is therefore the next A/Z subject index entry constructed by chain procedure?

Metallurgy	669.9	— frame 312
Metallurgy : Assaying	669	— frame 303
Metallurgy	669	— frame 297

---

294 (309)

Your answer: 656.7, ie Air transport management.

The analysis of this chain should be as follows:

6	Applied sciences
65	Management
656	Transport
656.7	Air

Surely each of the above steps of division is expressed in the class number 656.7.

There is no hidden link.

Please return to frame 309 and consider the question once more. Remember to consult the schedules carefully when carrying out your analyses.

---

295 (305)

Your answer:

Yearbooks: Civil engineering 624(058)

Well, you *could* employ this entry and it does conform to the procedure of chain indexing.

However, this choice implies a decision to index *all* form concepts *directly* whenever they occur in the chain of a subject.

If you pause to think of *all* the form concepts, and *all* the possible subjects presented in those form, you will soon realize that this policy would result in a massive and uneconomical number of rather unhelpful index entries.

Please return to frame 305 and read again the explanation of the use of *see references* and *blanket references*. Then select the correct answer to the question and proceed with the course.

296 (299)
Your answer:
     Assaying : Metallurgy : Chemical technology   669.9
True, this is an acceptable A/Z index entry for this subject. It leads with
the last term in the chain, qualifies this with superordinate terms and
provides the full class number for the subject.

However, we did say that the lead term should always be qualified by
the *minimum number of superordinate terms* required to indicate the
precise subject context.

In the above entry the use of the qualifying terms 'chemical technology'
can be regarded as redundant. They do not add anything of real value to
the specific subject statement,
     Assaying : Metallurgy   669.9
Please continue with the course on frame 293

---

297 (293)
Your answer:
     Metallurgy   669
Correct.

Metallurgy is a sought term in the chain and the next one we would
provide an index entry for. It does not require further qualification by
superordinate terms to indicate its precise context and is indexed to the
class number for this subject, ie to the class number appropriate to its
level in the chain, 669.

Here is the chain for class 669.9 again:
    6   Technology
    66   Chemical
    669   Metallurgy
    669.9   Assaying
We have now provided two A/Z subject index entries according to
chain procedure
     Assaying : Metallurgy   669.9
     Metallurgy   669
The same procedure is used in constructing entries for the other
potentially sought terms in the chain.

Write down what you consider to be the A/Z subject index entries
remaining to be constructed for this subject and then turn to frame 308.

298 (309)
Your answer: 656.1/.5 ie Land transport management.
The analysis of this chain should be as follows:
6	Applied sciences
65	Management
656	Transport
656.1/.5	Land

Surely each one of the above steps of division is expressed in the class number 656.1/.5.

Please return to frame 309 and consider the question once more. Remember to consult the schedules carefully when carrying out your analyses.

---

299 (291)
You should have arrived at the following analysis.

Class number 669.9

Chain	6	Technology
	66	Chemical
	669	Metallurgy
	669.9	Assaying

If you have a different answer check to see where you went astray. Have you omitted a step of division? Have you written down unnecessary terms from the schedules at any of the steps?

You are now ready to make the first A/Z subject index entry for this subject. This is the *specific A/Z subject index entry* as it directs the searcher *immediately* to the location of this specific subject in the classified file.

It is constructed by *leading* with the *last* term in the chain and qualifying this with the *minimum number of superordinate terms* necessary to indicate the precise subject context.

This verbal subject statement is indexed to the *full class number*.

Which of the following do you consider is the specific A/Z subject index entry for the subject represented by class number 669.9 constructed according to the above procedure?

Technology : Metallurgy : Assaying	669.9	– frame 304
Assaying : Metallurgy	669.9	– frame 292
Assaying : Metallurgy : Chemical technology	669.9	– frame 296

300 (315)

Your answer: the concept *'Senses'* constitutes a false link in the chain.
No, you are wrong.

The subject under consideration is *'The psychology of perception'*.
Your analysis of the chain should be as follows

1	Philosophy
159.9	Psychology
159.93	Senses
159.937	Perception

Surely the subordination of *'Perception'* to *'Senses'* could not be regarded as a case of *false subordination* in this conceptual chain.

Consequently 'Senses' does *not* constitute a 'false link' in the chain.

Please return to frame 315. Read what was said about false links again and then select another answer to the question.

---

301 (309)

Your answer 656.2 ie Railway transport management. Correct.

The analysis of this chain is as follows.

6	Applied sciences
65	Management
656	Transport
656.1/.5	Land
656.2	Railway

The step of division, 656.1/.5 Land transport, is not expressed notationally in the class number 656.2 and yet it constitutes one of the concepts in the chain of this subject.

It is therefore a *hidden link* in the chain and one that requires an A/Z subject index entry as follows:

Railway transport : Management	656.2
Land transport : Management	656.1/.5
Transport : Management	656
Management : Applied sciences	65
Applied sciences	6

Continue on the next frame

Inadequacies in the *specific A/Z subject index entry* made for a subject can also occur if the indexer bases his analysis solely on the *class number* for that subject.

The specific A/Z index entry must provide a verbal statement of the specific subject and direct the user *at once* to the location of this subject in the classified file.

It is constructed by *leading* with the *last* term in the chain.

Now suppose you classify the following document as stated below;

Title	*'Natural history of the Weald'*	
SA	Natural history/Gt Britain/Weald	
Class number	502(422)	
Chain	5	Science
	502	Natural history
	502(4)	Europe
	502(410)	Gt Britain
	502(420)	England
	502(422)	South-east

By leading with the last term displayed in this analysis we produce the index entry

South-east England : Natural history   502(422)

Does this index entry provide a verbal statement of the specific subject?

Yes   – frame 319

No   – frame 310

303 (293)
Your answer:

Metallurgy : Assaying 669

No. This is decidedly wrong.

The lead term 'metallurgy' is all right but you have then gone on to qualify this by the *subordinate* term in the chain 'assaying' and indexed this to the class number 669.

The resulting A/Z subject index entry is wrong on two counts.

1 The verbal subject statement repeats a citation order already present in the classified file.

2 The class number 669 is *not* the class number for the subject metallurgy : assaying. The correct class number for this subject is 669.9 and access to it has already been provided for in the specific A/Z subject index entry

Assaying : Metallurgy 669.9

Please return to frame 293 and read through the text again carefully; then select another answer to the question.

---

304 (299)
Your answer:

Technology : Metallurgy : Assaying 669.9

No. This is most definitely wrong.

You have chosen an entry which leads with the first term in the chain and then qualifies this by successively *subordinate terms.*

Your verbal statement thus follows the *same* citation order as the class number. If entries were constructed by this method the A/Z subject index would simply repeat an order of subjects already to be found in the classified file.

Please return to frame 299. Look at the chain and then read through the chain indexing procedure described once more. Then select another answer to the question.

The A/Z subject index entries you should have derived from this chain are given below.

    'Three-dimensional cinematographic projection'
    Class number 778.554.1
    Chain   7   Arts=Fine arts
                  77   Photography
                  778   (Special applications)
                  778.5   Cinematography
                  778.55   Film projection=Projection
                  778.554   (Special methods)
                  778.554.1 Stereoscopic=Three-dimensional

A/Z Subject index entries

Three-dimensional film projection	778.554.1
Stereoscopic film projection	778.554.1
Film projection	778.55
Projection : Cinematography	778.55
Cinematography	778.5
Photography	77
Arts, fine	7
Fine arts	7

Make sure that you have provided entries for synonyms and have omitted the unsought links in the chain.

The statement that all synonyms are indexed directly requires some qualification.

When the use of all synonymous terms as indexing terms would result in a massive, and thus uneconomic, duplication of A/Z subject index entries *see references* are employed to direct the user from the rejected term or terms to the chosen indexing term. In other words when the term represents a widely distributed concept.

Suppose, for example, that the indexer decides that the terms *'Great Britain'* and *'United Kingdom'* are to all intents synonymous. Then, instead of making all the many index entries required under Great Britain and repeating them under the term United Kingdom he would choose only one of these terms as an indexing term.

A *see* reference is then made from the rejected term to the chosen term, eg

    Great Britain   *see* United Kingdom

A similar procedure is adopted when dealing with *form concepts*. Information about almost every subject could be presented in the form of, say, a *report*.

If we were to index all the subjects about which reports were written under the lead term report it would generate a lengthy sequence of entries all filed under the same term. Instead, a large scale saving of index entries is achieved by producing a *general* or *blanket* reference in some such form as the following:

> Reports *see* names of individual subjects. The class number for the subject is subdivided by the notation (047) to indicate report.

Suppose you have to produce A/Z subject index entries by chain indexing procedure for the subject of the document '*A yearbook of civil engineering*'. The class number assigned is 624(058).

Analyse the chain of this class and then decide which of the following index entries you would employ.

> Yearbooks : Civil engineering   624(058)   – frame 295
> Yearbooks *see* names of individual subjects   – frame 314

---

306 (315)

Your answer: Philosophy. Correct.

After editing, the analysis of the chain for the subject 'The psychology of perception' 159.937 would thus be as follows:

1	(Philosophy)
159.9	Psychology
159.93	Senses
159.937	Perception

We can regard Philosophy as a *false link* in the chain. The subordination of the contemporary scientific discipline of Psychology to Philosophy could now be regarded as a case of *false subordination*.

We should not now expect a user, searching for information about the '*Psychology of perception*', to consult the index under Philosophy. This term would not therefore be indexed. Our edited chain would thus generate the following entries:

Perception : Psychology	159.937
Senses : Psychology	159.93
Psychology	159.9

Continue with the course on frame 320.

---

307 (311)

Your answer: Film projection.

Now if you think more carefully you must agree that someone searching for information about '*Three-dimensional cinematographic projection*' might consult the index under '*Film projection*'.

This then would *not* be considered an 'unsought' term in the chain.

An 'unsought' term is one which a user would rarely, if ever, think of consulting in the A/Z index when formulating his request for information about a particular subject.

Please return to frame 311 and reconsider the question. Then select another answer and proceed with the course.

You should have produced the following A/Z subject index entries:

    Chemical technology   66
    Technology   6

These two index entries provide for approaches via the two remaining sought terms in the chain and index each concept to its appropriate class number.

Let us now look at the completed set of A/Z subject index entries made by chain indexing procedure for the subject *'Select methods of metallurgical assaying'* :

Class number	669.9		
Chain	6	Technology	
	66	Chemical	
	669	Metallurgy	
	669.9	Assaying	
Index entries	Assaying : Metallurgy	669.9	
	Metallurgy	669	
	Chemical technology	66	
	Technology	6	

Continue on the next frame

We said earlier that the analysis of a class into its chain must always be carried out by consulting the *schedules* of the classification scheme.

This is to ensure that no important step of division, which may well represent a sought term, is omitted from the analysis.

As you know, concepts in chain order are in an order of successive subordination. They are arranged in a *hierarchical order.*

If the notation of a classification scheme is not strictly expressive of all hierarchical relationships, then it is possible that one, or more, of the concepts in the chain of a particular subject are *not* represented notationally in the class number for that subject.

Take, for example, the subject *'Christian dogma'.* The UDC class number for this subject is 23. By looking at this class number alone it would appear to have only two steps of division.

    2   Religion
    23   Dogma

However, if you consult the *schedules* for class 2 you will see that there are in fact *three* steps of division which go to form this class number for Christian dogmatics, namely:

    2   Religion
    22/28   Christian
    23   Dogma

The step of division, 22/28 Christian religion, is *not expressed notation-*

ally in the UDC class number 23.

It is, however, present in the *chain of the subject* represented by class number 23. This presence must be recognized, for it constitutes a sought term and must receive an A/Z subject index entry as follows:

Dogma : Christian religion   23
Christian religion   22/28
Religion   2

Steps of division which are not expressed in the class number, and yet constitute part of the chain, are known as 'hidden links' in the chain.

In order to ensure that all 'hidden links' are recognized in the analysis of a chain, this analysis must always be carried out by a careful consultation of the schedules, *not by reliance on the class number alone.*

Now consider the following three subjects and their respective UDC class numbers.

Air transport management   656.7
Railway transport management   656.2
Land transport management   656.1/.5

Analyse each of the subjects represented by these class numbers into their respective chains. Which one of these chains includes a hidden link?

656.7   – frame 294
656.2   – frame 301
656.1/.5   – frame 298

---

310   (302)
Your answer: the index entry

South-east England:Natural history   502(422)

does *not* provide a verbal statement of the *specific subject*.

You are right.

The subject of this document is *specifically* about the natural history of the *Weald* and so the specific A/Z subject index entry should be

Weald : Natural history   502(422)

However, the concept 'Weald' is *not* specified in the class number 502(422). An analysis of this class number, *as it stands*, would not reveal this concept in the chain and thus the specific subject would receive no A/Z index entry. Its existence would remain unknown to the user.

In order to ensure that we do in fact produce the specific A/Z index entry by chain procedure it is necessary to *extrapolate* (ie *extend*) the chain *verbally* as follows:

5   Science
502   Natural history
502(4)   Europe
502(410)   Gt Britain
502(420)   South-east
502(422)   Weald

The need to extend the chain verbally arises when the classification scheme is *insufficiently detailed* to provide a *specific class number* for the subject.

The situation will rarely arise with UDC *if* the scheme is applied to its *full capacity* by the use of verbal extensions to the class number itself.

Thus, in the example, Natural history of the Weald, the full UDC class number would be, 502 (422 Weald), giving us the chain,

5	Science
502	Natural history
502 (4)	Europe
502 (410)	Gt Britain
502 (420)	England
502 (422)	South-east
502 (422 Weald)	Weald

However, UDC is by no means *always* applied to this degree of detail in libraries. In such situations verbal extensions to the *chain* are essential to ensure effective A/Z subject index entries.

Moreover, this point is of importance as regards the general principles of chain indexing.

The analysis of the chain is the analysis of the *subject itself*, not simply of the class number.

The schedules must always be consulted to ensure that a *full* analysis of the class is achieved, that *every step of division* in the chain is stated.

We said earlier that each step of division should be stated, as far as is possible, by a *single word*. The adoption of this procedure simplifies the process of chain indexing. Use of the terms displayed in the schedules can prove unnecessarily confusing and can lead to inaccurate A/Z index entries.

Consider again the example *'Railway transport management'*, UDC class number 656.2.

In the analysis of this chain we encounter some of the *composite headings* frequently used in the UDC schedules.

Take, for example, the heading for class 656. You will see the following display in the schedules:

656   Transport and postal services

The concept 'postal services' is, in fact, specifically catered for at class 656.8:

656.8   Mail. Post.

This concept plays no part in the chain of the subject represented by class number 656.2 *'Railway transport management'*.

It should be omitted from the analysis of the chain, thus:

656   Transport

Composite headings abound in UDC. When dealing with them you should always select the concept relevant to the chain you are analysing and express this, as far as possible, by a single word.

The copying of words and phrases from the schedules encourages the indexer to use them as they stand and so produce index entries under which the user would not think of looking. Not all classification schemes employ terms in their schedules that are intended as *indexing terms* for retrieval purposes.

An obvious example occurs in the Colon Classification in class 2, Library science, where the term in the schedules for 'special libraries' is *'business'*. No user would look under 'business libraries' when searching for information about 'special libraries'.

Such adjustments to terminology are best made in the initial analysis of the chain.

A more likely fault to arise from copying phrases out of the schedules is the construction of A/Z index entries which contravene chain indexing procedure.

Look, for example, at UDC class *343.19 Criminal courts and tribunals.* This verbal display in the schedules *might* lead to the A/Z index entry

Criminal courts   343.19.

However, as a sub-class of 343, Criminal law, we require the entry

Courts :Criminal   343.19

To help ensure this entry, employing the desired citation order, the term 'courts' only should be used in the analysis of the chain at class 343.19.

Some concepts, of course, can only be expressed by more than one term, eg *'Current affairs'*. There is no single term which adequately expresses this concept.

Nevertheless, as a *general rule* for the analysis of a chain, the use of more than one term at any single step of division should only be tolerated if these terms are more or less synonymous. We shall return to the problem of synonyms shortly.

For the above reasons, we repeat that each step of division should be stated, as far as possible, by a *single word* in the analysis of a chain.
Continue on the next frame

311 (310)
The procedures mentioned so far have been directed towards a *complete analysis* of the chain of any given class. By following them, your initial analysis of a chain should be a full analysis and it should be written down in a form that helps to ensure effective and helpful A/Z index entries.

Obviously, A/Z subject index entries are only made if they help the user locate the desired subject in the classified file.

To ensure further that all the index entries generated by chain procedure are indeed helpful, the initial analysis of the chain *may* require *EDITING.*

This editing of the chain takes place *before* any A/Z subject index entries are made.

The analysis of a subject into its chain may well reveal one or more steps of division representing terms that would rarely, if ever, be consulted by a user looking for information about that subject.

These are referred to as *unsought terms* ie *not* liable to be consulted or 'sought', by a user.

Consider the following subject and its chain:

'Three-dimensional cinematographic projection'

Class number	778.558.1	
Chain	7	Arts
	77	Photography
	778	Special applications
	778.5	Cinematography
	778.55	Film projection
	778.554	Special methods
	778.554.1	Stereoscope

Which of the following steps of division represents in your opinion an unsought term in this chain?

Cinematography	– frame 318
Special methods	– frame 316
Film projection	– frame 307

---

312 (293)
Your answer:

Metallurgy 669.9

This is incorrect.

True, we do require an index entry for the term 'metallurgy', but to what class number do we index this term?

669.9 is *not* the class number for metallurgy. It represents the more specific subject *metallurgical assaying.*

Remember that, in each A/Z subject index entry, the verbal subject statement is indexed to its appropriate class number.

Please turn to frame 293 and read through the text again carefully; then select another answer to the question.

313 (315)
Your answer: the concept *'Psychology'* constitutes a false link in the chain. No, you are wrong.

The subject under consideration is *'The psychology of perception'*.
Your analysis of the chain should be as follows:

1	Philosophy
159.9	Psychology
159.93	Senses
159.937	Perception

The subordination of *'Senses'* to *'Psychology'* could hardly be regarded as a case of *false subordination* in this conceptual chain.

Consequently, 'Psychology' does *not* constitute a 'false link' in the chain.

Please return to frame 315. Read what was said about false links again and then select another answer to the question.

---

314 (305)
Your answer:
Yearbooks *see* names of individual subjects
Correct.

In other words you would employ a *general* or *blanket reference* from a term denoting a form concept ie 'Yearbooks'.

Remember that *see* references are only used in the A/Z subject index when they result in a large scale saving of index entries.

The general rule is to index synonyms *directly*. By doing so we provide *direct* access to the classified file via all synonymous terms liable to be consulted by the user.

For this reason the recognition of synonyms is one of the procedures in the editing of the chain.
Continue on the next frame

315 (314)

The final aspect of editing the chain that we must consider is the recognition of any step of division manifesting a case of *false subordination.*

When a concept is falsely subordinated to another this must be regarded as a *fault* in the classification schedules.

Such faults might arise from a poor organization of the schedules, or a mistake in the initial conceptual analysis or a failure to recognize a generally accepted change in the relationship between concepts.

Whatever the reason, a step of false subordination, revealed in the analysis of a chain, is referred to as a *false link* in the chain.

As such they would not be sought by a user looking for information about the specific subject and they would not receive index entries.

Consider the subject *'The psychology of perception'*, class number 159.937.

Analyse this class by reference to the schedules and then say which of the following concepts constitutes a false link in the chain in your opinion.

Senses	— frame 300
Psychology	— frame 313
Philosophy	— frame 306

---

316 (311)

Your answer: Special methods.

Correct. It is highly unlikely that any one would consult the A/Z subject index under the term 'Special methods'. This would therefore be regarded as an *unsought link* in the chain and would receive no index entry.

In fact this particular chain contains *two* unsought links. Having analysed the chain these would be noted in its editing by, for example, enclosing them in brackets as illustrated below.

This editing helps to ensure that the unsought links, or unsought terms, do *not* receive index entries and are *not* employed as qualifying terms.

Class number	778.554.1	
Chain	7	Arts
	77	Photographic
	778	(Special applications)
	778.5	Cinematography
	778.55	Film projection
	778.554	(Special methods)
	778.554.1	Stereoscopic

Continue on the next frame

This particular chain provides examples of another form of editing—the recognition of *SYNONYMS*.

The policy in the construction of the A/Z subject index is to index all synonymous or near synonymous terms *directly*. That is, we do not generally choose one term as an indexing term and then *refer* the user from synonymous terms to entries under the chosen term.

The use of such *see references* from a synonym to a preferred indexing term is restricted as it saves the user from having to consult *two* parts of the A/Z subject index *before* he is able to gain access to the classified file.

For example, taking the two terms *Disease* and *Pathology* we make such index entries as the following

Disease : Medicine 616

Pathology : Medicine 616

By providing index entries under *both* terms, the user can gain access to classified file directly by consulting either one of the terms.

He is *not* referred from, say, Pathology to Disease by the reference

Pathology *see* Disease

before he can gain access to the relevant part of the classified file.

As we intend to provide A/Z subject index entries for synonymous terms, synonyms are indicated in the analysis of the chain by further editing.

This form of editing can be done by writing synonyms at their appropriate level of the chain and introducing them with an = (equals) sign.

Look again at the following chain. It has now been edited to recognize *unsought links* (in brackets) and *synonyms* (introduced by =).

'Three-dimensional cinematographic projection'

Class number 778.554.1

Chain		
	7	Arts = Fine arts
	77	Photography
	778	(Special applications)
	778.5	Cinematography
	778.55	Film projection = Projection
	778.554	(Special methods)
	778.554.1	Stereoscopic = Three-dimensional

Now write down what you consider to be the A/Z subject index entries derived from this edited chain. Then turn to frame 305.

318 (311)

Your answer: Cinematography.

Surely it is feasible that a person searching for information about the subject *'Three-dimensional cinematographic projection'* might consult the index under the term *'Cinematography'*.

If this is so then *'Cinematography'* would *not* be considered an 'unsought' term in the chain.

Remember that an 'unsought' term is one which a user would rarely, if ever, think of consulting in the A/Z index when formulating his request for information about a particular subject.

Please return to frame 311 and reconsider the question. Then select another answer and proceed with the course.

---

319 (302)

You think that the index entry provides a verbal statement of the specific subject. You must reconsider your decision.

The index entry in question is

South-east England : Natural history   502(422)

It is true that this provides a specific verbal statement of the subject expressed in the class number. But is it a verbal statement of the specific subject about which the document is written?

It is of vital importance that you do not confuse the two. In analysing a chain we are analysing a *subject*, not a class number.

Please return to frame 302. Look, more carefully, at the subject of the document. Then reconsider the question and proceed with the course.

---

320 (306)

The foregoing discussion of chain indexing has been set in the context of a classified catalogue employing, as a general rule, a *single specific subject entry* in the classified file for each document, ie a *single entry system.*

Other systems are used, especially in classified catalogues employing UDC, but these will not be dealt with in this particular volume.

It was not our intention, nor indeed is it feasible, to cover every eventuality that will be encountered in producing A/Z index entries for the subjects of particular documents by chain indexing procedure.

You have, however, been introduced to the fundamental principles of chain indexing and, from the basis of this understanding, you should be in a position to deal with most of the problems liable to arise in practice.

We shall now summarize the main points made in the second part of this section of the course. You will then be required to produce A/Z subject index entries by chain procedure for the subjects of particular documents on your own.

SUMMARY

1 The analysis of a chain is the analysis of a *subject* not simply of a class number.

2 The analysis of a chain must therefore be carried out by a careful consultation of the *schedules* of the classification scheme.

3 This is to ensure that a *full analysis* is achieved, that *every step of division* is stated, including any

    a) *Hidden links*—intermediate steps of division not expressed in the class number.

    b) *Extensions to the chain*—where the class number is *not specific.*

4 Every step of division should be stated, as far as possible, by a *single term.*

5 This full analysis of the chain may then require editing in order to identify

    a) *Unsought links*—these *will not* receive index entries.

    b) *False links*—these *will not* receive index entries.

    c) *Synonyms*—these *will* receive index entries.

6 A/Z subject index entries can now be made for every term in the edited chain which is liable to be *sought* by a user looking for information about the specific subject.

7 In each case the lead term is qualified by the *minimum number* or necessary *superordinate terms* and is indexed to the class number appropriate to its level in the chain.

(NB: Once an A/Z subject index entry has been made for a particular subject it need *never again* be repeated.)

This fact tends to be lost sight of when considering chain indexing in isolation from the construction of an actual catalogue.

In this course, however, you are *not* concerned with the construction of an actual catalogue. Your concern is to practice the technique of chain indexing. You must treat each subject as a *separate entity* and produce A/Z subject index entries accordingly.

Continue on the next frame

As a conclusion to these sections dealing with the classified catalogue we offer the following exercise in the application of chain indexing procedure.

You have already provided a subject analysis and a UDC class number for each of the two following examples and these are repeated here for convenience.

1 *'Cereal diseases :Ministry of Agriculture, Fisheries and Food Bulletin No 129'*
SA: Agriculture/Cereals/Diseases
UDC 633.1-2

2 *'Library resources in the Greater London area :No 5 Agricultural libraries'*
SA: Library science/Special libraries/Agriculture/London
UDC 026:63(421)

For each of the above subjects would you now produce:

a) an analysis of the chain

b) A/Z subject index entries by chain indexing procedure

Check your answers with those provided on frame 350.

SECTION 6: THE ALPHABETICAL SUBJECT CATALOGUE

In the previous section of this course we were concerned with the classified catalogue. This type of catalogue consists, traditionally, of *three* separate parts—the author/title index, the classified file, and the A/Z subject index to the classified file.

The classified catalogue facilitates the retrieval of information about subjects through:

1. a classified arrangement of subjects in the classified file;
2. access to, and support of, this classified arrangement via the names of subjects arranged in alphabetical order in the A/Z subject index.

We must now turn our attention to the *alphabetical subject catalogue*. This type of catalogue, as its name implies, provides for the retrieval of information about subjects by *naming* subjects in *verbal statements* and arranging these subject names in *alphabetical order*.

There is *no* classified sequence of subjects in the alphabetical subject catalogue. It is often said that the basic theory of the alphabetical subject catalogue is the utility to the user of providing *direct access* to the *'known names'* of subjects (ie verbal statements) in a *'known order'* (ie alphabetical order). This, as we shall see, is a considerable oversimplification of the problem.

The problems of alphabetical subject cataloguing can be, and often are, demonstrated by reference to the *dictionary catalogue*.

The dictionary catalogue derives its name from the fact that it consists of a *single sequence* of entries and references filed in alphabetical order of headings.

All types of entry and reference—author, title, subject, series etc—are *interfiled* in this one sequence which thus caters for *all* approaches to information retrieval.

In this particular course we are only concerned with catalogues as tools for the retrieval of information about named subjects, ie the 'subject approach' to information retrieval. We are not therefore concerned with the dictionary catalogue in its totality.

Many 'dictionary' catalogues are, in fact, 'divided'. This is, the author/ title entries and references are filed in a separate sequence from the subject entries and references. These subject entries and references thus constitute an *alphabetical subject catalogue*.

From now on we shall refer exclusively to the alphabetical subject catalogue, named, for convenience, the *A/Z subject catalogue*.

In a library using an A/Z subject catalogue, a classification scheme is only used to determine the classified order of documents on the shelves. It is not used directly for the arrangement of document representations in the catalogue. The A/Z subject catalogue possesses no classified sequence of entries as is found in the classified file of a classified catalogue. It is composed entirely of entries and references arranged in an alphabetical order of subject names.

Subject cataloguing for the A/Z subject catalogue thus involves two fundamental activities:

1 the selection of *verbal subject headings* under which the entries for individual documents will file;

2 the construction of a system of *subject references* (cross-references) which is designed to guide the user from one subject heading to related subject headings under which relevant information, in the form of document entries, can be found. This makes up for the absence of a systematic sequence showing such connections.

The core problem, and the first with which we shall deal, is the selection of the *subject heading* for a document entry, ie the name of the subject about which the document is written.

Continue on the next frame

---

323 (322, 333)
SUBJECT HEADINGS

The subject heading under which the entry for a particular document files should be a *specific* description of the subject about which that document is written.

It is thus called a *specific subject heading.*

If a user consults the A/Z subject catalogue, *at his first approach*, under the specific subject heading which describes the subject of his search he will *immediately* discover what documents the library possesses containing information about that subject. The document entries filed under this subject heading contain the call marks for these documents telling the user where they can be located in the classified shelf arrangement.

For example, if the user wants information about *Town planning* and he consults the catalogue under this subject heading he will find there entries for documents about town planning, eg:

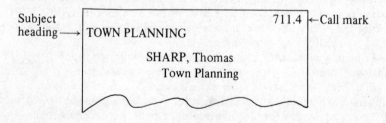

Subject heading⟶ TOWN PLANNING   711.4 ←Call mark

SHARP, Thomas
Town Planning

Unlike the classified catalogue, where the user must first consult the A/Z subject index (only *references*) and *then* go to the classified file of *full entries*, the A/Z subject catalogue theoretically provides *direct access* to entries for documents about named subjects.

However, to achieve this *direct* access, the user must locate the relevant specific subject heading at his *first* approach to the catalogue.

This assumes that he has formulated his request by:

1 naming the subject at the *specific level* desired;
2 naming this specific subject *in the same terms* used by the indexer;
3 citing these terms *in the same order* as they are cited in the specific subject heading.

Unless *all* these conditions are observed, access to a subject in the A/Z subject catalogue is *not direct* and a further search must be made via a *subject reference* of some kind. We shall deal with the problem of references later.

Now the majority of subject headings are statements of *compound subjects*. Such compound subject headings are composed of more *than one term*. As soon as we have more than one term in a heading, the decision as to the citation order of those terms is one of critical importance.

Obviously the *first cited term*, ie the *lead term* in the heading, determines where the subject heading will file in the alphabetical sequence of subjects and thus where it can be located.

The aim of a subject heading is that it should name the subject in the form *most likely to be sought by* a user.

However, in the case of many compound subjects there is *no* such obvious form of name. There is no *'known name'*.

Consider, for example, the subject *'The advertising of aluminium pressure-cookers on television'*.

This subject consists of the four elements

Advertising : Aluminium : Pressure-cookers : Television.

There is no *accepted name* for a compound subject such as this. There is no obvious *citation order* for its constituent terms. Different enquirers might ask for this subject in quite different ways—eg, is there anything on *TV advertising of aluminium pressure-cookers?*

As we saw in the A/Z subject index to the classified catalogue, the attempt to provide for every possible approach to the citation order of terms in compound subjects by permuting the terms may lead to an unacceptable number of entries in the catalogue.

We must therefore attempt to select the chosen form of name ie the chosen form of the specific heading in the case of the A/Z subject catalogue.

As there are no rules in natural language that allow us to predict the one 'accepted' or 'sought' name for many compound subjects, we must inevitably look for other rules.

E J Coates, former editor of the British Technology Index (now the Current Technology Index), has suggested a *'significance order'* of terms which helps us to determine the citation order in headings for compound subjects, at least up to a point.

This order is based on the *conceptual relationships* between the constituent elements of a compound subject.

You are already familiar with the idea that concepts can be regarded as manifestations of particular categories of concepts, eg Ranganathan's five Fundamental Categories P M E S T.

Coates uses different names for categories of concepts and suggests that the basic *significance order* is the citation order of categories Thing ⟶ Material ⟶ Action. To this we can add the category Agents, giving us a *basic significance order* of

Thing ⟶ Material ⟶ Action ⟶ Agent

This must be supplemented by further rules for less obvious relations, but the above will take us a long way in solving the problem of citation order. However, it should be noted that such a significance order of categories is more readily recognizable in, and applicable to, the disciplines of natural science and technology than to the social sciences, humanities and fine arts.

Now if we take that compound subject *'The advertising of aluminium pressure-cookers on television'* and cast its constituent concepts in the basic *significance order* Thing ⟶ Material ⟶ Action ⟶ Agent, we arrive at the following citation order:

Thing	*Material*	*Action*	*Agent*
Pressure-cooker :	Aluminium :	Advertising :	Television

In this particular subject pressure-cookers constitute the 'Thing', aluminium the 'Material', advertising the 'Action', and television the 'Agent' through which the advertising is carried out.

Consider the subject *'Application of computers to the quality control of wool textiles'*.

If we cast the constituent concepts of this compound subject in the basic significance order of Thing ⟶ Material ⟶ Action ⟶ Agent, at which of the following citation orders do we arrive?

Wool : Textiles : Quality control : Computers   – frame 331
Textiles : Wool : Quality control : Computers   – frame 328
Computers : Textiles : Wool : Quality control   – frame 334

Your answer:

    Occupational diseases : Diagnosis.

Correct.

In this compound subject 'occupational disease' is the *Thing*, 'diagnosis' is an *Action*. Consequently, by following the *significance order* we arrive at the above subject heading.

If we had adhered strictly to the citation order prescribed by *chain procedure*, ie *lead* with the *last term* in the chain, qualified by *superordinate* terms, we would have produced the subject heading

    Diagnosis : Occupational diseases

Neither of these headings is 'incorrect'. There is no 'correct' way of naming a compound subject such as this.

The indexer's guiding principle is to produce a subject heading in the form 'most likely to be sought be a user'.

This factor undoubtedly introduces an element of subjectivity on the part of the indexer in his selection of the citation order of terms in a compound subject heading.

In the above example he must decide which of the headings is most likely to be sought by the user and there is no law to guide him.

In your practical indexing in this course, the procedure you are required to follow in the selection of specific subject heading is this:

1   Follow the citation order prescribed by *chain procedure*, ie lead with the last term in the chain qualified by superordinate terms.

2   Modify this order *only* when you think it generates a decidedly *unhelpful* subject heading.

3   In such cases use the *basic significance order* Thing ⟶ Material ⟶ Action ⟶ Agent as your guide in determining the modified citation order of the compound subject heading.

As we have said, this procedure involves a definite element of subjectivity in deciding just what is the most helpful citation order.

However, once having made this decision, an essential factor is to ensure that the system of *subject references* leads the user to the chosen form of subject heading.

It is in the construction of a system of references that chain procedure really plays a vital role and it is to this problem that we now turn our attention.

Continue with the course on frame 339.

325 (344)
Your choice:

Diseases : Diagnosis *see also* Diagnosis : Diseases

No, you are wrong.

This answer implies that you have used the heading

Diagnosis : Diseases

under which to make entries for particular documents about this subject.
If there were no document entries under a heading you would not direct
a user to it via a *see also* reference.

If fact you have rejected this particular heading in favour of one employing the citation order

Diseases : Diagnosis

Please return to frame 344. Look at the example carefully, then choose
the correct answer to the question.

---

326 (332)
You think that if we suppress a term in the specific subject heading then
the citation order in that heading follows the order prescribed by chain
procedure.

No, this is not true.

Remember that the citation order prescribed by chain procedure is a
citation order that leads with the last term in the chain.

If we *suppress* or *subordinate* a term in specific subject heading we
remove that term from its lead position. We remove it from the position
prescribed by strict adherence to chain procedure order.

Please return to frame 332. Read through the text carefully and look
at the example again. Then select the correct answer to the question and
continue with the course.

---

327 (329)
Your answer:

Metallurgy : Assaying

is the specific subject heading derived by chain procedure.

How can this be? Metallurgy is not the *last* term in this chain. The
last term in the chain is Assaying and you have used this term to *qualify*
Metallurgy.

Please return to frame 329. Read again about chain procedure in the
selection of the *citation order* in compound subject headings. Then select
another answer to the question and proceed with the course.

328 (323)
Your answer:

Textiles : Wool : Quality control : Computers.

Correct. This represents the basic significance order:

Thing $\longrightarrow$ Material $\longrightarrow$ Action $\longrightarrow$ Agent

applied to the compound subject 'Application of computers to the quality control of wool textiles'.

Textiles are the Thing, wool the Material, out of which the Thing is made, quality control the Action and computers the Agent through which the Action is carried out.

The basic significance order is not sufficiently detailed to provide precise rules for the citation order in *all* compound subjects. For example we may well have more than one manifestation of the categories Thing, Material, Action or Agent in a given compound subject.

Coates has further refined this basic significance order by defining some twenty types of relationships between concepts in compound subjects and giving the suggested citation orders based upon these relationships. [See Coates, E J 'Subject catalogues: headings and structure'. Library Association, 1960.]

For the purposes of this course we do not intend to use this detailed analysis of citation orders based on the relationship between categories of concepts.

We shall base our procedure for the construction of subject headings upon the conceptual relationships expressed in *classification schemes*. This, however, is only one method available for the systematic selection of headings and we shall return to the basic significance order Thing $\longrightarrow$ Material $\longrightarrow$ Action $\longrightarrow$ Agent later.

Continue on the next frame

---

329 (328)
CONSTRUCTION OF SUBJECT HEADINGS BY CHAIN PROCEDURE

It is possible to utilize the conceptual relationships expressed in a classification scheme in the selection of subject headings for document entries in the A/Z subject catalogue, ie in the naming of subjects about which the documents are written.

This method has the important added advantage, as we shall see, of providing a system of *subject references* as well as giving us a citation order for compound subject headings.

In our practical indexing we shall concentrate upon this method and the classification scheme we shall refer to is UDC.

The technique is analogous to that already described for the construction of A/Z subject index entries in the classified catalogue and is similarly based upon *CHAIN PROCEDURE*.

Having classified a document, the class to which the document has been assigned is analysed into its *conceptual chain*.

Remember that this is an analysis of the *subject* itself, not of the class number as it stands.

The analysis of the chain must be a *complete* analysis with every step of division stated.

This complete analysis *may* then require various forms of *editing*.

These procedures have been dealt with in the previous section of this course and will not be restated here.

The *specific subject heading* is then constructed in a way very similar to that employed in constructing the specific A/Z subject index entry for a classified catalogue by chain indexing procedure.

The *last* term in the chain provides the *lead term* (ie the first cited term) in the specific subject heading.

This is qualified by the *minimum number of superordinate terms* necessary for a precise statement of the specific subject.

Let us consider again our fairly straightforward example *'Select methods of metallurgical assaying'*, UDC class number 669.9.

Chain: 6   Technology
        66   Chemical
        669   Metallurgy
        669.9   Assaying

Which of the following is the specific subject heading for this subject derived by chain procedure?

Metallurgy : Assaying   — frame 327
Assaying : Metallurgy   — frame 332
Assaying   — frame 335

---

330 (337)
Your answer:

Slavery : Abolition *see* Abolition : Slavery

No, this reference would *not* appear.

You have modified chain procedure order and *rejected* the heading Abolition : Slavery.

Then why make a *see* reference *from* a preferred *to* a rejected form of heading?

Return to frame 337 and read through the text once more. Then carefully consider the example before selecting the correct answer to the question.

331 (323)
Your answer:
    Wool : Textiles : Quality control : Computers.
No, this is not correct.
    In this subject context the concept wool plays the role of Material. It
is the Material of which the Thing is constituted.
    If this is so then your citation order cannot conform to the basic signi-
ficance order
        Thing ⟶ Material ⟶ Action ⟶ Agent
    Please return to frame 323 and reconsider the question.

---

332 (329)
Your answer:
        Assaying : Metallurgy
Correct. This specific subject heading has been constructed by leading
with the last term in the chain and qualifying this with the superordinate
term 'metallurgy'. This verbal statement is sufficient to give us a precise
statement of the specific subject.
    Strict adherence to the citation order prescribed by chain procedure
can sometimes produce an obviously unhelpful citation order of terms in
a compound subject heading.
    For example, if the *last* term in the analysis of the chain represents a
time or *form* concept, then by strict adherence to chain procedure, this
would constitute the *lead* term in the subject heading.
    However, entry under a time or form concept would rarely be helpful
to the user and in such cases these terms are subordinated in the subject
heading.
    Take, for instance, the subject of the document *'Conference proceedings
on secondary education'.*

UDC class number	373 (063)	
Chain	3	Social sciences
	37	Education
	373	Secondary
	373 (063)	Conference proceedings

    If we were to adhere strictly to the citation order prescribed by chain
procedure, ie lead with the last term in the chain, we should arrive at the
subject heading
        Conference proceedings : Secondary education
    A much more helpful citation order for the subject heading is, however,
        Secondary education : Conference proceedings
    In other words we have *suppressed* the terms 'conference proceedings'
in order to achieve a more helpful subject heading which leads with the
terms 'secondary education'. (It may be remembered that such terms as
'Conference proceedings' do appear in the A/Z Subject Index to a classified

file—but only as *general references*, eg Conference proceedings on particular
subjects *see* name of subject.)

If, as in the above example, we suppress a term in the specific subject
heading which of the following statements is true?

The citation order in the subject heading follows
that prescribed by chain procedure.　　　　　　— frame 326

The citation order in the subject heading
modifies that prescribed by chain procedure.　　— frame 338

333　(338)

You say that the basic significance order referred to is

Agent $\longrightarrow$ Action $\longrightarrow$ Material $\longrightarrow$ Thing

No. In fact this is the *reverse* of the basic significance order.

You should return to frame 323 and do some revision on the basic
significance order.

Then continue with the course on frame 340.

334　(323)

Your answer:

Computers : Textiles : Wool : Quality control.

No, this is not so.

In this particular subject context computers do not constitute a Thing.
They could represent this category in other subjects, eg *'The manufacture
of computers'*, where they are the Thing being manufactured. In the
subject in question, however, they represent an Agent facilitating the
carrying out of an Action, namely quality control.

Thus your citation order cannot conform to the basic significance
order:

Thing $\longrightarrow$ Material $\longrightarrow$ Action $\longrightarrow$ Agent

Please return to frame 323 and reconsider the question.

335　(329)

Your answer:

Assaying

is the specific subject heading derived by chain procedure.

Assaying is the last term in the chain but it does not, by itself, provide
a description of the *specific subject*. This is the aim of a *specific subject
heading*.

Please return to frame 329 and read carefully through the text once
more. Then choose the correct answer to the question and proceed with
the course.

336 (339)
Your answer:

     Higher education *see also* Education
     Education   *see also* Social sciences

No, this is an incorrect answer.

You were asked to select the references that lead *from* broader *to* narrower subjects.

Surely 'Higher education' is *narrower* in extent than 'Education' and 'Education' narrower than 'Social sciences'

Therese are not therefore references that lead from broad subjects to narrower, more specific ones.

Please return to frame 339 and read through the text again, looking at the examples carefully. Then select the correct answer and proceed with the course.

---

337 (344)
Your answer:

     Diagnosis : Diseases *see* Diseases : Diagnosis

Quite right.

The chosen specific subject heading modifies the citation order pre-scribed by chain procedure. We must therefore provide a *see* reference *from* the rejected form of heading *to* the chosen form of heading.

If we failed to provide this see reference, the sought term in the chain 'Diagnosis' would not appear as a lead term in the system of references generated for the specific subject.

The rule thus established is, if the specific subject heading represents a *modification* of the citation order prescribed by chain procedure, then a *see* reference must be made *from the rejected heading*, ie that one prescribed by chain procedure, *to the chosen heading*.

Now the need to modify chain procedure order does not only occur at the last step in a conceptual chain, ie in the creation of the specific subject heading.

This need may arise at any one of the superordinate steps in the chain, ie in the creation of any one of the see also references leading to that heading.

Strict adherence to chain procedure may produce an unhelpful citation order in any of the subject headings corresponding to superordinate steps in the hierarchy.

At whatever step you decide to modify chain procedure order to produce a more helpful heading, you must ensure that a *see* reference is made from the rejected to the chosen form of heading.

Consider, for example, a document about *'The abolition of slavery in the USA'*.

     UDC class number   326.8(73)

The conceptual chain of this class is analysed below. The full subject heading corresponding to each step in this chain is provided as the preliminary stage in the construction of a *specific subject heading* and a series of *specific references.*

326.8(73)

3	Social sciences	Social sciences
32	Political science	Political science
326	Slavery	Slavery
326.8	Abolition	Slavery : Abolition
326.8(73)	USA	Slavery : Abolition : USA

Which of the following references would appear in the system of references constructed?

Slavery : Abolition *see* Abolition : Slavery   — frame 330

Abolition : Slavery *see* Slavery : Abolition   — frame 346

---

338   (332)

You say that the citation order in the subject heading *modifies* that prescribed by chain procedure. You are quite correct.

Chain procedure tells us to *lead* with the *last* term in the chain. This would give us the subject heading:

Conference proceedings : Secondary education.

However, we consider that a more helpful subject heading is:

Secondary education : Conference proceedings.

By choosing this more helpful heading, which *suppresses* the form concept 'conference proceedings', we have altered, or *modified*, the citation order prescribed by chain procedure. We have *not* lead with the last term in the chain.

The practice of modifying the citation order prescribed by chain procedure can be extended beyond the suppression of time and form concepts to any situation in which the indexer considers that this citation order produces an unhelpful subject heading.

When such a case arises in your practical indexing you are required to use the basic significance order, mentioned earlier, as a guide in determining the modified chain order.

The basic significance order based on categories of concepts is:

Agent $\longrightarrow$ Action $\longrightarrow$ Material $\longrightarrow$ Thing   — frame 333

Thing $\longrightarrow$ Material $\longrightarrow$ Action $\longrightarrow$ Agent   — frame 340

CONSTRUCTION OF SUBJECT REFERENCES BY CHAIN PROCEDURE

So far we have only considered the problem of selecting a specific subject heading. It is under the chosen form of heading that the catalogue entry for a particular document is filed and hence located.

However, unless a searcher looking for information about a specific subject formulates his request

1 at the *specific level* desired,
2 using the *same terms* as the indexer has used,
3 citing these terms in the *same order* as they are cited in the specific subject heading,

he will be unable (at least at first) to locate the relevant subject heading in the catalogue. He will not be able to retrieve documents relevant to his request.

Moreover, there is no *classified* arrangement of subjects in the A/Z subject catalogue. The order of *names* of subjects arranged alphabetically, is a relatively *arbitrary* order so far as bringing together related topics is concerned. Many of the most important relations will be completely lost (eg Tigers will file a long way from Cats). Since the showing of relationships by juxtaposition is relatively poor, the display is dependent to a large extent on *references*, or *cross-references*.

There references are of two kinds:

1 those linking related subject headings under *both* of which entries for documents have been made
in the form 'Subject X *see also* Subject Y'
2 those *leading* from subject headings which have been *rejected* for the purpose of document entry (but which the user may still think of consulting) *to* subject headings under which entries have have made
in the form 'Subject X *see* Subject Y'

Chain procedure provides a systematic method of selecting *see* and *see also references* which will guide the searcher to the specific subject heading he desires and indicate related headings.

The user may well formulate his request at a more general, less specific level than that of the subject he actually requires. We encountered this when dealing with the classified catalogue.

For example, when searching for information about the subject *'Metallurgical assaying'* he may consult the catalogue under the term *'Metallurgy'* while the specific subject he wants has been entered under the heading

Assaying : Metallurgy

There is no classified sequence of subjects which will lead him from metallurgy to the sub-class *assaying : metallurgy* in the A/Z subject catalogue. We must provide him with a *see also* reference.

Chain procedure allows us to select a series of *see also* references from broader to narrower subjects ('general to special').

These are made <u>one step at a time</u> from *superordinate* to *subordinate* terms in the chain. This of course assumes that both terms are 'sought' terms.

In each case the lead term in the subject statements is qualified by the minimum number of superordinate terms necessary to indicate its *precise* context. If this qualification is *not* observed we will produce only *generalized* series of references—connections between *specific* headings will not be made.

To ensure that this does not occur write down the *full subject heading* corresponding to *each step in the chain.* Then construct your *see also* references from these headings, not from the single terms used in your initial analysis of the chain.

eg	Subject	*'Select methods of metallurgical assaying'*	
	Class number	669.9	
	Chain	6	Technology	Technology
		66	Chemical	Chemical technology
		669	Metallurgy	Metallurgy
		669.9	Assaying	Assaying : Metallurgy

The specific subject heading for this subject is,

Assaying : Metallurgy

We now make a series of see also references, one step at a time from broader to narrower subjects culminating in the specific subject heading thus:

Technology	*see also*	Chemical technology
Chemical technology	*see also*	Metallurgy
Metallurgy	*see also*	Assaying : Metallurgy

Now consider the following subject of a document entitled,

'The role of higher education'

Class number   378

Chain	3	Social sciences	Social sciences
	37	Education	Education
	378	Higher	Higher education

Specific subject heading   Higher education

Which of the following series of references is from broader to narrower subjects?

Higher education	*see also* Education	
Education	*see also* Social sciences	– frame 336
Social sciences	*see also* Education	
Education	*see also* Higher education	– frame 341

340 (323, 338)
Correct. The basic significance order referred to is
    Thing ⟶ Material ⟶ Action ⟶ Agent
If we decide to *modify* the citation order prescribed by chain procedure to produce a subject heading regarded as more helpful to the catalogue user, then this *significance order* can be employed as a guide in determining the modified citation order.

Consider *'Notes on the diagnosis of occupational diseases'*. Let us suppose you classify this document by UDC as follows:

    Class number 616-057-07
    Chain   6   Applied science
                  61   Medicine
                  616   Disease
                  616-05   Environmental
                  616-057   Occupational
                  616-057-07   Diagnosis

If you produce a subject heading employing the significance order
Thing ⟶ Material ⟶ Action ⟶ Agent, which of the following headings would you arrive at?

    Diagnosis : Occupational diseases   – frame 345
    Occupational diseases : Diagnosis   – frame 324

---

341 (339)
Your answer: the following series of references leads from broader to narrower subjects:

    Social sciences *see also* Education
    Education   *see also* Higher education

Correct. These have been constructed, *one step at a time*, from *superordinate* to *subordinate terms* in the chain. This has produced a series of *see also* references leading from broader to narrower subjects culminating in the specific subject heading

    Higher education

The making of a series of *see also* references from qualified *subordinate* to qualified *superordinate* terms in the chain, ie from *narrower* to *broader* subjects (*'special to general'*) is very simply done using the same chain structure, eg

    Higher education *see also* Education
    Education   *see also* Social sciences

However, in most A/Z subject catalogues such references are omitted purely on grounds of economy.

In view of the frequency with which users could benefit from references to a broader subject this omission must be regarded as a deficiency of A/Z subject catalogues.
Continue on the next frame

342 (341)

See also references from subjects *related* to the specific subject *but not present in the chain structure of that subject* can also be helpful to the searcher.

Such related subjects may appear in fairly widely separated parts of the classification schedule however, eg,

Social geography *see also* Town planning

The selection of such references is very much at the discretion of the indexer and as yet no firm rules have been developed to guide him in his choice.

For the purposes of this course, you must concentrate on *see also* references derived from the conceptual chain of the specific subject, leading one step at a time from qualified superordinate to qualified subordinate terms. These are the traditionally used general to special references leading from broader to narrower subjects and culminating in the specific subject heading.

Continue on the next frame

---

343 (342)

We must finally consider the use of *see* references derived by chain procedure.

These are the references which direct the searcher *from rejected headings to the chosen headings* under which entries for documents have been made.

You will recall that time and form concepts are usually *suppressed* in a subject heading. Thus *'A dictionary of medicine'* would be entered under the heading

Medicine : Dictionaries

This is regarded as a more helpful subject heading than the one produced by strict adherence to the citation order prescribed by chain procedure, ie

Dictionaries : Medicine

We must still provide for the user who consults the catalogue under the terms representing form concepts however.

We make this provision by *blanket* or *general* references similar to those employed in the A/Z subject index in the classified catalogue, eg

Dictionaries on special subjects *see* Names of individual subjects,
eg Medicine : Dictionaries

The same procedure is adopted for time concepts. Direct entry under a time concept is both wasteful and unhelpful in most subjects and thus we use a blanket reference, eg

History of individual subjects *see* Names of the individual subjects.

Continue on the next frame

In the A/Z subject catalogue entries for individual *documents* are made under the chosen subject heading.

It is thus uneconomical and wasteful of space in the catalogue to provide entries for documents under *all synonymous* subject headings.

Consequently the practice is to select one term as an indexing term, ie, to be used for document entry. The user is then referred *from* synonymous terms to the chosen terms under which entries have been made.

For example, we might select *Cardiovascular system* as an indexing term for use in subject headings and reject the synonym *Circulatory system*.

We must then provide the following see reference for the benefit of the user who consults the catalogue under the rejected term:

Circulatory system *see* Cardiovascular system

You are already aware that the recognition of synonyms is one of the processes in editing a chain.

When synonyms occur, *see* references must be made *from* the rejected term, or terms, *to* the chosen indexing term.

A most important kind of *see* reference generated by chain procedure is that made from a *rejected specific subject heading* to the *chosen specific subject heading*.

If we modify the citation order prescribed by chain procedure when selecting the specific subject heading for a compound subject we, at the same time, *reject* a specific subject heading in the alternative, less helpful citation order, ie that one prescribed by strict adherence to chain procedure.

It is essential to direct the user *from* the rejected subject heading *to* the chosen subject heading. We do this by a *see* reference.

Consider a document about *'The diagnosis of diseases'*.

UDC class number   616-07
Chain   6   Applied sciences
                           61   Medicine
                           616   Diseases
                           616-07   Diagnosis

The chosen specific subject heading is *Diseases : Diagnosis*.

Having selected this heading, which of the following references would you employ?

Diseases : Diagnosis *see also* Diagnosis : Diseases   − frame 325

Diagnosis : Diseases *see*   Diseases : Diagnosis   − frame 337

345 (340)
Your answer
     Diagnosis : Occupational diseases.
No, this is a wrong decision.

     In this compound subject the concept 'Diagnosis' is an *Action* performed
on 'Occupational diseases'.

     Therefore your citation order does *not* follow the basic significance order
          Thing ⟶ Material ⟶ Action ⟶ Agent
     Please return to frame 340. Read again about the *modification* of chain
procedure order, look carefully at the example, then select the correct answer
to the question and proceed with the course.

---

346 (337)
Your answer:
     Abolition : Slavery *see* Slavery : Abolition
Correct.

     We have modified chain procedure order to produce the heading
Slavery : Abolition. We must therefore provide the *see reference* from the
rejected form of heading. This ensures that the sought term in the chain,
Abolition, occupies the *lead position* in a reference.

     In this instance we have also modified chain procedure order to produce
the *specific subject heading.*
     Slavery : Abolition : USA
The *space* concept has been suppressed in the heading. In many subjects space is thus suppressed in specific subject headings although this is
not such a general rule as the suppression of form or time. In some subjects, eg History, Geography, space occupies a primary role and entry
under these concepts may well be helpful. This may also apply in certain
of the Social sciences and entry under space is very much at the discretion
of the indexer.

     However, the modifications to chain procedure order decided upon in
this example, might lead the indexer to make the following references.
     Slavery *see also* Slavery : Abolition
     Slavery : Abolition *see also* Slavery : Abolition : USA
Having once directed the user to the heading *Slavery* it is reasonable to
expect him to search *all* the entries under this term and its subheadings.

     Consequently these two references would usually be omitted. They
would only be provided if the number of entries filed under Slavery and
its subheadings was very large.

     We should, of course, still require the see reference from the rejected
specific subject heading.
     USA : Slavery : Abolition *see* Slavery : Abolition : USA
     Let us look finally at the edited chain and the specific subject heading
and references derived from it.

Subject   *'The abolition of slavery in the USA'*
Class no 326.8 (73)

Chain			
	3	Social sciences	Social sciences
	32	Political science=Politics	Political science
	326	Slavery	Slavery
	326.8	Abolition	Slavery : Abolition
	326.8(7/8)	(Americas)	
	326.8(7)	(North America)	
	326.8	USA=United States of America	Slavery : Abolition : USA

Specific subject heading   Slavery : Abolition : USA

References

Social sciences	*see also*	Political science
Political science	*see also*	Slavery
Abolition : Slavery	*see*	Slavery : Abolition
USA : Slavery : Abolition	*see*	Slavery : Abolition : USA
Politics	*see*	Political science
United States of America	*see*	USA

The guiding principle is always that the system of *see* and *see also* references directs to user to the specific subject heading chosen for the subject. Continue on the next frame

---

347 (346)

Chain procedure, or, more precisely, *modified chain procedure,* is by no means the *only* method of deriving subject headings and references for the A/Z subject catalogue. It is, however, the one examined for the purposes of this course and it does provide a systematic method of:

1 selecting a subject heading which is a *specific description* of the document's summarized subject content;

2 economically generating a series of *see* and *see also* references which lead the user to this specific subject heading by providing an entry point in the catalogue for each term in the chain reflecting the different hierarchical levels of a user's approach to the subject.

We shall now briefly summarize the main points regarding modified chain procedure and then you will be required to employ this method for yourself.

SUMMARY
1 Having classified a document, analyse the class assigned into its complete conceptual chain and edit this chain as required.
2 Write down the *full subject heading* corresponding to each sought link in this edited chain.
3 Construct the *specific subject heading* by leading with the last term in the chain, qualified by the minimum number of superordinate terms.
4 *Modify* this order *only* if you think that, by doing so, you produce a more helpful specific subject heading.
5 When modifying chain procedure order use the *basic significance order* Thing $\longrightarrow$ Material $\longrightarrow$ Action $\longrightarrow$ Agent as your guide.
6 These last two points apply equally to the selecting of subject headings corresponding to superordinate steps in the chain.
7 Construct a series of *see also* references leading *one step at a time* from broader to narrower subjects and culminating in the chosen specific subject heading.
8 Construct *see* references from *synonyms* and from *rejected forms of compound subject headings.*
9 Check to ensure that the system of references directs the user to the chosen specific subject heading and that all *sought terms* in the chain appear as lead terms in this system of references.
Continue on the next frame

---

348 (347)
Having now concluded our consideration of the A/Z subject catalogue, we suggest that you try the following exercise in applying modified chain procedure to the construction of subject headings and references.

Earlier in the course you provided a subject analysis and a UDC class number for each of the following examples. These are repeated here for convenience.

1 *'Therapy through hypnosis'*
   SA   Medicine/Therapeutics/Hypnotherapy
   UDC 615.851.2

2 *'Roots of contemporary American architecture: a series of essays'*
   SA   Architecture/Contemporary/American/Essays
   UDC 72.036(73)(04)

For each of the above subjects would you now produce:
   a) an analysis of the chain
   b) a specific subject heading and a series of subject references by
      modified chain procedure

Check your answers with those provided on frame 351.

349 (268)

Answers to the examples set in frame 268.

1 *'Library resources in the Greater London area: No 5 Agricultural libraries'*
   SA   Library science/Special libraries/Agriculture/London
   UDC   026:63(421)

2 *'Therapy through hypnosis'*
   SA   Medicine/Therapeutics/Hypnotherapy
   UDC   615.851.2

This class number is enumerated for you in the index although it does not occur in the schedules of the abridged UDC (see the index entry Hypnosis and then its subheading of psychotherapy). This is, therefore, an instance where the index provides you with a more specific class number than is enumerated at the appropriate part of the abridged schedules themselves. The class number so provided in such cases is correct and should be used.

However, if you have consulted the index under the entry for, say, Psychotherapy itself, you will only have the lead to class 615.851. If you have then constructed a compound class number by subdividing 615.851. by the concept hypnotism you should have arrived at

615.851:159.962

3 *'Cereal diseases: Ministry of Agriculture, Fisheries and Food Bulletin No 129'*
   SA   Agriculture/Cereals/Diseases
   UDC   633.1-2

4 *'Roots of contemporary American architecture: a series of essays*
   SA   Architecture/American/Contemporary/Essays
   UDC   72.03(73)6(04)

In this discipline Space and Time together form the Style facet and, as such, constitute 'Personality' concepts. The above citation order is achieved by the intercalation of (73). You may well have employed the citation order

Architecture/Contemporary/American/Essays

where Time precedes space in the formation of the Style facet. Translated, this citation order gives the UDC class number

72.036(73)(04)

5 *'The selected poems of Robert Graves'*
   SA   Literature/English/Poetry/Robert Graves/Selections
   UDC   820-1 Graves 3

We hope that, if your answers diverged from the above solutions, you are able to appreciate why the divergence occurred.

A potential area of difference is obviously in the choice of citation order. In UDC there is no 'correct' citation order. Thus, when providing instruction in the use of the scheme, it is necessary to conform to some guiding principle in this choice. We have employed PME...ST as just such a general guide.

We do not imply that this citation order is the one that should be used in relation to UDC in all contexts.

The important point to appreciate is that the indexer must decide on a citation order and adhere to it when classifying by UDC.

Your knowledge of UDC will be drawn upon in the following sections of this course. If you feel, therefore, that there are parts of the preceding sections you could usefully revise, this is the time to do so.

Resume the course on frame 269.

350 (321)

Answers to the examples set on frame 321.

1 *'Cereal diseases:Ministry of Agriculture, Fisheries and Food Bulletin No 129'*

SA Agriculture/Cereals/Diseases

UDC 633.1-2

Chain 6   Applied sciences
    63   Agriculture
    633 Crops
    633.1 Cereals
    633.1-2 Diseases

A/Z subject index entries

Diseases : Cereals : Agriculture	633.1-2
Cereals : Agriculture	633.1
Crops : Agriculture	633
Agriculture	63
Applied sciences	6

2 *'Library resources in the Greater London area: No 5 Agricultural libraries'*

SA Library science/Special libraries/Agriculture/London

UDC 026:63(421)

Chain 0   (Generalities)
    02   Librarianship=Library science. Libraries
    026   Special libraries
    026:6   (Applied sciences)
    026:63 Agriculture
    *026:63(4) Europe
    *026:63(41-4) UK
    *026:63(420) England
    026:63(421) London

A/Z subject index entries

London : Agricultural libraries	026:63(421)
Agricultural libraries	026:63
Special libraries	026
Libraries	02
Librarianship	02
Library science	02

*whether or not to make entries under England, UK and Europe is at the discretion of the indexer. In many situations they would probably be regarded as unnecessary.

Please proceed with the course in frame 322.

Answers to examples set on frame 348.

1 *'Therapy through hypnosis'*

SA   Medicine/Therapeutics/Hypnotherapy

UDC   615.851.2

Chain			
	6	Applied sciences	Applied sciences
	61	Medicine=Medical sciences	Medicine
	615	Therapeutics	Therapeutics : Medicine
	615.8	(Physiotherapy)	
	615.85	(Various treatments)	
	615.851	Psychotherapy	Psychotherapy
	615.851.2	Hypnotherapy	Hypnotherapy

Subject heading   Hypnotherapy

References

Applied sciences	*see also*	Medicine
Medicine	*see also*	Therapeutics : Medicine
Therapeutics : Medicine	*see also*	Psychotherapy
Psychotherapy	*see also*	Hypnotherapy
Medical sciences	*see*	Medicine

2 *'Roots of contemporary American architecture: a series of essays'*

SA   Architecture/Contemporary/American/Essays

UDC   72.036(73)(04)

Chain			
	7	Arts=Fine arts	Fine arts
	72	Architecture	Architecture
	72.03	(Style)	
	72.036	Contemporary=Modern	Contemporary architecture
	72.036(7/8)	(The Americas)	
	72.036(7)	(North America)	
	72.036(73)	USA=United States of America	USA : Contemporary architecture
	72.036(73)(04)	Essays	

Subject heading   USA : Contemporary architecture : Essays

References

Fine arts	*see also*	Architecture
Architecture	*see also*	Contemporary architecture
Contemporary architecture	*see also*	USA : Contemporary architecture
Essays		General reference
Modern architecture	*see*	Contemporary architecture
United States of America	*see*	USA

Please continue on the next frame.

You have now completed these sections concerned with the UDC, the classified catalogue and the A/Z subject catalogue.

The objectives of this part of the course could be stated in the following terms:

Having produced a specific summarization of the subject content of a document cast in PME...ST citation order, you should be able

1 to translate this subject analysis into a UDC class number following your citation order as far as the scheme allows.

2 to produce entries for this subject, by chain indexing procedure, for the A/Z subject index to a single entry system classified catalogue employing UDC.

3 to produce, by modified chain procedure based on UDC, a specific subject heading and a system of references for this subject in an A/Z subject catalogue.

Such a statement of objectives may appear narrowly defined in its practices and yet, at the same time, rather sweeping in its assumptions. Some amplification is therefore desirable to place it in its full context.

It was not our aim, nor indeed is it feasible in a course of this nature, to make the reader highly proficient in all aspects of classification with UDC and in all methods employable in the construction of subject catalogues. We selected certain procedures, the appreciation of which we consider of fundamental importance in understanding the use of classification schemes and the structure of subject catalogues. On the other hand, to claim total competence in the application of even these selected skills to all subjects expressable in documents obviously requires a breadth of knowledge and a degree of practice lying far beyond the capabilities of a course such as this to inculcate.

These objectives should thus be viewed as part of the wider intent of the course. Through practice in these particular procedures, we have attempted to acquaint you with a set of basic principles that will help you to classify documents and produce entries in subject catalogues with an awareness of the structure and limitations of the tools you are using, an appreciation of your ultimate objective and thus an ability to obtain this end more efficiently.

As a concluding exercise we suggest you apply the *total* process of subject analysis, classification by UDC and the provision of catalogue entries by chain procedure to each of the two following examples:

1 *'Teachers in higher education in the United Kingdom: an official report'*

2 *'The education of women in India: a bibliography'*

For both these examples produce
- a) a subject analysis at the level of specific summarization, cast in a PME...ST citation order.
- b) a UDC class number following your citation order as far as the scheme allows.

For the subject of example 1, produce a series of entries for an A/Z subject index to a classified catalogue by chain indexing procedure.

For the subject of example 2, produce a specific subject heading and a system of references for the A/Z subject catalogue, by modified chain procedure.

Check your answers with the solutions suggested below.

Answers

1 *'Teachers in higher education in the United Kingdom: an official report'*

SA	Education/Higher/Teachers/UK/Report
UDC	378.12 (41-4) (047)

Chain		
	3	Social sciences
	37	Education
	378	Higher
	378.1	(General organization)
	378.12	Teachers
	378.12(41-4)	UK=United Kingdom
	378.12(41-4)(047)	Reports

A/Z subject index entries

Reports General reference	
UK : Teachers : Higher education	378.12(41-4)
Teachers : Higher education	378.12
Higher education	378
Education	37
Social sciences	3
United Kingdom *see* UK	

2 *'The education of women in India: a bibliography'*
  SA   Education/Women/India/Bibliography
  UDC   371.04-055.2(540):016
  Chain   3   Social sciences   Social sciences
          37   Education   Education
          371   (Teaching etc)
          371.04   (with reference to pupil)
          371.04-055.2   Women   Women : Education
          371.04-055.2(540)   India   India : Women :
                                                      Education :
          371.04-055.2(540):016 Bibliographies   India : Women
                                                      Education :
                                                      Bibliographies

Subject heading India : Women : Education : Bibliographies
References
  Bibliographies   General reference
  Social sciences   *see also* Education
  Education   *see also* Women : Education
  Women : Education *see also* India : Women : Education

In the next section we are going to consider an approach to subject indexing different from the methods looked at previously. If your answers are
therefore divergent from the ones suggested here it might be wise to
revise certain points made in the foregoing text before continuing. The
areas of divergence will suggest the points to revise.

Continue on the next frame

SECTION 7: POST-COORDINATE INDEXING

Before we proceed to examine the principles of post-coordinate indexing it is advisable to recapitulate some of the main features inherent in the approach to subject indexing already discussed.

In our consideration of subject indexing so far, in the classification of documents each document has been assigned to a class which constitutes a *summarization* of its total subject content.

In the majority of cases, ie wherever the subject of a document is a compound subject, the description of this class contains *several elements*. These elementary constituents of compound subjects have been synthesized, or combined, in a *preferred citation order*, to form the index description of the compound class.

This combination has taken place at the *stage of indexing* the document or at the *stage of input* into the system.

The elements of compound subjects are said to have been *COORDIN-ATED* at the *indexing stage* of the document.

Probably the simplest way of illustrating what has happened is by referring to the following diagram.

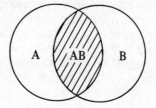

In the above diagram, A represents that class of documents in the library dealing in some way with concept A. B represents that class of documents dealing in some way with concept B.

For 'concept' may be read any relatively elementary term such as Libraries, Staff, Buildings, Recruitment, Chemistry.

The *intersection* of classes A and B represents class AB which thus contains documents that are about the interaction of A and B. It is a *compound class.* A typical intersection might be *Recruitment (of) Staff.*

This intersection of classes is called the *COORDINATION* of classes. This coordination has taken place at the stage of indexing a document and therefore it has taken place *before* any particular request is placed for information about the compound subject of the document, eg *Staff Recruitment.*

The subject description is composed of a set of terms which constitutes a summarization of the subject.

The assumption is that this subject description reflects a likely way in which the information concerned will be asked for. Thus, when a user asks for information on a particular compound subject, the combination of concepts involved will be easily matched in the index against an entry for the same combination.

Because this method of indexing *coordinates* the elements of compound subjects *before* any particular request is placed for information on that particular compound it is known as *PRE-COORDINATE* indexing.

Now which of the following statements do you consider to be true?

In the classification of documents and in the construction of indexes so far in this course you have been following the method of pre-coordinate indexing   — frame 358

In the classification of documents and in the construction of indexes so far in this course you have not been following the method of pre-coordinate indexing   — frame 355

---

354 (369)

You say that the coordination of concepts has taken place at the indexing stage. No, you are wrong.

If we had coordinated the concepts at the indexing stage we should have provided an index description of the compound subject *'Computer cataloguing in libraries'*.

We did not do this. We indexed only the three elementary constituents of this compound — Cataloguing, Computers and Libraries.

Before continuing with the course you should return to frame 353 and revise what was said there about the coordination of concepts.

Then go to frame 369, read through the text carefully, select the correct answer to the question and proceed with the course.

355 (353)

You think that you have *not* have been following the method of pre-coordinate indexing so far in this course. You must reconsider your answer.

Whenever you have classified the compound subject of a document and subsequently provided index entries, in either the classified or A/Z subject catalogue, for that subject, you have combined the constituent elements of the compound in a preferred citation order.

This process of combination has thus taken place at the indexing stage of the document, before any request has been placed for information about the compound subject.

Please, therefore, return to frame 353. Consider carefully the explanations of the *coordination* of concepts and of why *pre-coordinate* indexing is so-called. Then select the correct answer and proceed with the course.

---

356 (369)

You say that the coordination of concepts has taken place at the *search stage.* You are correct.

By this method only simple subject concepts are indexed. These concepts are not coordinated — ie their *intersection* to form a compound subject is not revealed until the search stage. That is at the stage of *output* from the system.

Because this coordination of concepts does not take place until after a request is placed for information about a particular compound subject, this method of indexing is called *POST-COORDINATE*, or often simply *COORDINATE INDEXING.*

In its early stages, as exemplified by Uniterm, post-coordinate indexing employed subject concepts *as they were expressed in the document* for the index description of that document.

Although indexing can thus be performed in 'natural language', ie by using keywords taken directly from the document, in very many cases post-coordinate indexing now involves the use of a *controlled vocabulary* of indexing terms.

Such a controlled vocabulary forms the basis of an *indexing language* which is used both at the indexing and search stages of a post-coordinate indexing system.

Which of the following statements do you consider true?

Post-coordinate indexing does not usually include
the translation stage of indexing — frame 360
Post-coordinate indexing does usually include the
translation stage of indexing — frame 370

You say you would expect to find the instruction

    PROGRAMMED INSTRUCTION

        BT Teaching methods

Correct. This entry under the term Programmed Instruction indicates that the term Teaching methods is a *broader term* (BT), ie at a higher level in the generic hierarchy.

    Terms related in other than genus/species relationships, eg Thing/Action, Action/Agent, are usually indicated separately by using the comprehensive direction.

    RT (= *Related Term* ie a non-genus/species relationship)

    The relationship between the concepts Wheat and Harvesting is a relationship between a Thing and an Action performed on that Thing.

    Which of the following thesaurus entries under the term Wheat is correct?

    WHEAT

        BT Harvesting   – frame 363

    WHEAT

        RT Harvesting   – frame 368

    WHEAT

        NT Harvesting   – frame 371

You say that in the classification of documents and in the construction of indexes so far in this course you have been following the method of pre-coordinate indexing. You are correct.

Whenever you have provided an index description of a compound subject, either in notational or verbal terms, you have combined the constituent elements of that compound in a preferred citation order.

The *coordination* of concepts has thus taken place at the indexing stage of the document, *before* any request is placed for information about the compound subject of the document. This is *pre-coordinate* indexing.

Pre-coordinate indexing, by indexing compound subjects in this way — combining several elements in a single summary description and citing these elements in a preferred order — gives rise to the central problem in the retrieval of those subjects, *distributed relatives.*

You first encountered the problem of distributed relatives when considering the structure of the classified catalogue.

In our consideration of this catalogue we examined a *single entry system.* In a single entry system each document is, as a general rule, provided with a single specific subject entry in the classified file. A series of A/Z subject index entries can then be generated by chain indexing procedure.

You saw that chain indexing provides a very economical and a very systematic method for the selection of those A/Z subject index entries. Nevertheless, it fails to overcome completely the problem of distributed relatives.

Suppose, for example, that the concept *computers* constitutes a distributed relative in the classified file by virtue of the preferred citation order employed in the classification scheme.

Chain indexing will generate a sequence of A/Z subject index entries *each of which* leads with the term *computers.* To this extent it will provide for the collocation of information about this concept in the A/Z subject index.

eg   Computers: Cataloguing: Co-operation: Public libraries Class no
      Computers: Cataloguing: Public Libraries   Class no
      Computers: Public Libraries   Class no

However, as you can see from the above example, if a searcher requires information on the subject *'Computers in Public Libraries'*, he must scan *the total number of entries* under the term computers to ensure that he has located *all* the potentially relevant information.

The reason for this is that the qualifier, Public Libraries, is *randomly* distributed depending on whether other facets are cited in between.

In a large file this can obviously prove very inconvenient.

Distributed relatives are inevitable in the *shelf arrangement* of documents but we can go some way towards alleviating the problem in catalogues. The best remedy for distributed relatives in catalogues is to be found in *MULTIPLE ENTRY SYSTEMS.* These we will now briefly examine.

When looking at the classified catalogue, we examined a single entry system because this demonstrates the fundamental principles of catalogue construction and of chain indexing.

Although, in a single entry system, there is a certain degree of collocation of distributed relatives in the A/Z subject index, these related concepts remain seriously scattered in the classified file.

In order to improve collocation in the *classified file* it is necessary to file entries under *each* of the elements in a compound subject. Thus if a document deals with subject AB, full entries are made under *each* of the constituent elements of this subject — one entry under AB, one under BA.

This results in *multiple entry in the classified file.* We must stress that this is in fact common practice in classified catalogues employing UDC. UDC is a scheme well suited to multiple entry systems since the major elements in a compound class number may be clearly displayed by the separating : (colon).

Of course we must still *select* from all the possible *permutations* of these elements when making multiple entries in the classified file for the majority of compound subjects of documents.

One frequently adopted method is known as *cycling.* By this method the constituent elements of a compound class number can be thought of as being on a wheel. Different permutations are made by reading the elements in a clockwise direction and leading with a different element in each compound. The notation is said to be *cycled.*

This can be conveniently demonstrated by using letters in place of actual UDC notation, eg:

Compound class number with 5 elements : ABCDE

Entries in the classified file produced by cycling : ABCDE
BCDEA
CDEAB
DEABC
EABCD

If we consider each of these elements as 'major' concepts, it will be seen that those scattered (distributed) in the classified file of a single entry system — B, C, D and E — are collected in a multiple entry system. By virtue of cycling, *each* of these concepts will appear in the *lead position* (ie the first cited concept) in entries for *all compound subjects* of which they are a constituent element.

Although this method increases the number of entries in the classified file, the number of A/Z subject index entries is ultimately reduced. Only the individual elements of each compound subject need now receive A/Z index entries.

eg	*Entries in the classified file*	*A/Z subject index entries*	
	Class number	Term	Notation
	ABCDE	a	A
	BCDEA	b	B
	CDEAB	c	C
	DEABC	d	D
	EABCD	e	E

Providing that the user can locate any *single concept* in the classified file, he will find there *all* the information relating to that concept.

Suppose, however, that the searcher requires information about the *compound subject* AC. True, he can find all the information about A *or* C filed at one point in the classified file.

Nevertheless, he will still have to search all the entries filed at one or the other of these points to ensure that he has located everything of relevance to the compound subject AC.

The system does not succeed in providing direct access to the location of *any* given compound subject in the classified file, only to some.

The same basic problems arise, of course, in the verbal description of compound subjects for retrieval purposes either in the A/Z subject catalogue or in the A/Z subject index to the classified catalogue. (For descriptions of multiple entry systems, eg PRECIS, see Foskett, A C *Subject approach to information*, 4th edn, Bingley, 1982.)

The root of the problem lies in the simple rule of the number of possible *combinations* in which a given set of concepts may be sought.

For example, a request for information about the subject *'Computer cataloguing in public libraries'* might be formulated as, 'Have you anything on . . . ',

> *Public library* cataloguing with computers?

or *Computer* cataloguing in public libraries?

or *Cataloguing* with computers in public libraries?

The formula for the total number of *combinations* in which a given set of terms may be sought is $2^n - 1$, where n is the number of terms in the set.

J R Sharp has suggested that, for indexing purposes, we can effectively *select* from this *total number* of possible combinations. (See Sharp, John R *Some fundamentals of information retrieval*, Deutsch, 1965.) For example, the topic ABC, consisting of three terms may be asked for in any of the following *seven combinations*,

> A
> AB
> ABC
> AC
> B
> BC
> C

However, if an entry is made under ABC, then the search for AB and A is

automatically catered for. These entries need not therefore be made.
Similarly, if an entry is made under BC, then we need no entry under B.
The minimum number of entries we need for ABC is not seven but
four. These are

ABC
AC
BC
C

The system of indexing devised by Sharp is known as SLIC — Selective
Listing in Combination.

The formula for predicting the number of selected combinations of
terms required is $2^{(n-1)}$.

Thus, if we have a compound subject consisting of three terms, ABC,
the actual number of combinations required for indexing purposes is

$2^{(3-1)} = 2^2 = 4$

However, even with selective indexing in combination, the limit of
feasibility is usually reckoned to be compound subjects consisting of five
terms. These subjects will generate sixteen entries in all and multiple
entry beyond this point is neither economically nor even physically
feasible in traditional forms of index.

Please continue on the next frame.

359 (358)
Since the early 1950s an approach to subject indexing has been developed
which attempts to overcome the problems of distributed relatives resulting
from the use of preferred citation orders in the index descriptions of
compound subjects.

This method differs from pre-coordinate indexing in principle, in the
physical forms of indexes which it generates and in the mechanics of
searching these indexes. The method is probably best appreciated by
examining it in its earliest and simplest form, the *UNITERM* index. In
the Uniterm index each individual index card represents a *simple* subject
concept.

A verbal description of this concept forms the *heading* on each card.
The index cards are thus usually arranged in the file in A/Z order of these
headings. Each *document* in the collection is given an *accession number*
on acquisition. The documents are then arranged on the shelves according
to this numerical order. They are *not* arranged in a classified order.

The subject analysis of each document for indexing purposes involves
the selection of *simple subject concepts* treated within that document.

For example, if we take a document dealing with the compound subject
Computer cataloguing in libraries, the subject analysis of this document
could consist of the three simple concepts
>COMPUTERS
>CATALOGUING
>LIBRARIES

The accession number of this document, let us say 123, is then entered on
each of the three index cards representing these three simple concepts.
Thus the compound subject of the document receives an index description
consisting of three concepts entered individually in the index.

Which of the following statements do you consider to be true?

In the Uniterm index, the compound subjects of
documents are indexed as compound subjects   — frame 364
In the Uniterm index, the compound subjects of
documents are not indexed as compound subjects — frame 369

---

360 (356)
You think that post-coordinate indexing does *not* usually include the
translation stage of indexing. This is untrue.

If the process of indexing includes the use of an *indexing language* then
it must also include the stage of *translation* into this indexing language.

Please return to frame 356 and read again what was said about post-
coordinate indexing and indexing languages. Then select the correct
answer to the question and proceed with the course.

361 (370)
Your answer: Post-coordinate indexing is the preferred term.
    No, this is not so.
    In a thesaurus the direction *use* directs you from a rejected term *to* a preferred indexing term. This may be a synonym, a near-synonym or a variant word form.
    If you therefore find the entry under Post-coordinate indexing,
        POST-COORDINATE INDEXING   *use*
        COORDINATE INDEXING
you are directed to use Coordinate indexing instead of Post-coordinate indexing. The latter is thus a *rejected term*.
    Conversely, under the *preferred indexing* term you will find the direction UF (= Use For) followed by the rejected term or terms.
    In this case, under the preferred indexing term Coordinate indexing you find the entry
        COORDINATE INDEXING
        UF Post-coordinate indexing
Now please proceed to frame 365 and continue with the course.

---

362 (365)
Your answer: PROGRAMMED INSTRUCTION
                NT Teaching methods
No. You should not expect to find the above entry in a thesaurus.
    The instruction NT means *Narrower Term*.
    This entry therefore indicates that Teaching methods is a *narrower term* than Programmed Instruction.
    This is not true as Programmed Instruction is a species of the genus Teaching methods and is therefore *higher* in the generic hierarchy than Programmed Instruction.
    Please return to frame 365. Read again about generic relationships and their display in a thesaurus. Then select the correct answer to the question and proceed with the course.

363 (357)
Your answer: WHEAT
                BT Harvesting
No. You would not expect to find this entry in a thesaurus.

The direction BT, (Broader Term), indicates that Harvesting is a broader term than Wheat.

We said that BT indicates terms that are higher in the generic hierarchy, ie related in the genus/species relationship.

Wheat is *not* a species of the genus Harvesting and therefore the relationship between these terms should *not* be indicated by the direction BT.

Please return to frame 357. Read through the text once more then consider the question carefully and select another answer.

---

364 (359)
You think that, in the Uniterm index, compound subjects are indexed as compound subjects.

You must reconsider your answer.

The subject of the document *'Computer cataloguing in libraries'* is a compound subject.

In the Uniterm index, however, this compound subject was indexed according to its three constituent isolate concepts Computers, Cataloguing and Libraries. We did not provide a *single index description* of the compound subject such as, Libraries: Cataloguing: Computers.

Please return to frame 359 and read through the description of the Uniterm index once more. Then select the correct answer to the question and proceed with the course.

---

365 (361, 370)
You say that *coordinate indexing* is the preferred indexing term. You are right.

You have received the instruction,
        COORDINATE INDEXING
            UF Post-coordinate indexing
This tells you to *use* Coordinate indexing *for* Post-coordinate indexing. A reverse instruction is thus located under the term Post-coordinate indexing,
        POST-COORDINATE INDEXING *use*
        COORDINATE INDEXING
Both at the indexing and search stages, as will be seen, it is valuable to have *relationships* between indexing terms displayed. Under each of its preferred indexing terms a thesaurus therefore lists *related terms*.

Terms representing concepts related in a genus/species relationship are usually indicated by the following instructions:

BT = *Broader Term*, ie *higher* in the generic hierarchy, *more general*
NT = *Narrower Term*, ie *lower* in the generic hierarchy, *more specific*
Thus the relationship between the terms *Libraries* and *School Libraries* would be displayed in a thesaurus by the following entries,

SCHOOL LIBRARIES
   BT Libraries
LIBRARIES
   NT School Libraries

A School library is one kind, or species, of Library. The genus/species relationship existing between these terms is indicated at their respective entries in the thesaurus.

We are told that Libraries is a *broader term* (BT) than School libraries and that School libraries is a *narrower term* (NT) than Libraries.

Programmed Instruction is a species of the genus Teaching methods.

Which of the following entries would you expect to find in a thesaurus?

PROGRAMMED INSTRUCTION
   NT Teaching methods   – frame 362
PROGRAMMED INSTRUCTION
   BT Teaching methods   – frame 357

---

366 (372)
Your answer: Objectives x Youth.

No. You have certainly broadened the search by using the genus in place of one of its species.

However, we said that a more effective method of broadening a search was to use the genus *and* species of that genus.

Please return to frame 372. Reconsider the question carefully then select another answer and proceed with the course.

---

367 (379)
Your answer: Students
              Opinions

No. This index description would not ensure the greatest *precision* in the retrieval of the document in question.

If we use the above description we are not sure whether the document is about the opinions *of* students or the opinions *towards* students.

Please return to frame 379. Read again what was said about the pre-coordination of terms. Then reconsider the question, select the correct answer and proceed with the course.

368 (357)
Your answer: WHEAT
              RT Harvesting.
Correct. We use here the comprehensive direction RT (= Related Term) to
indicate that there is a relationship, but a non-genus/species relationship,
between the concepts Wheat and Harvesting.

To fulfil adequately and consistently its role of displaying relationships,
a thesaurus should be based upon a prior analysis of the subject field with
which it deals and of the relationships between the constituent concepts
of this subject.

A faceted classification scheme is probably the most effective form of
such an analysis. At least for its generic relationships a thesaurus should
be based upon such a classification—as exemplified by the English Electric
'Thesaurofacet' referred to earlier.

Please continue on frame 372.

---

369 (359)
Your answer: In the Uniterm index, the compound subjects of documents
are not indexed as compound subjects. Correct.

Thus the index description of each document consists of a number of
simple subject concepts each indexed individually as an *isolate concept.*

In our example of the document about *'Computer cataloguing in libraries'* the index description consisted of three simple concepts,
      COMPUTERS
      CATALOGUING
      LIBRARIES
We did not provide an index description of the compound subject such as,
      LIBRARIES : CATALOGUING : COMPUTERS
In a Uniterm system, therefore, compound subjects are not indexed by
compound descriptions. There is no question of stringing together simple
concepts in a preferred citation order to produce a single index description
of the summarized subject content of a document.
In such a system, no one concept is subordinated to (and therefore distributed under) another as the result of using a preferred citation order.

If we index compound subjects in this way then how do we retrieve
information about them? Again this can be demonstrated by reference to
the Uniterm system. When a request is placed for information about a
compound subject, the elementary concepts constituting that compound
are searched for *individually.* The cards representing these elements are
retrieved from the file.

Consider again our document about *Computer cataloguing in libraries.*
This received the accession number 123 and was indexed under the terms
Computers, Cataloguing and *Libraries.* The three Uniterm cards would
appear like the following.

CATALOGUING

1	2	3	4	5	6	7	8	9	0
111	22	33	74	15	126	27	118	49	10
261	72	83	94	85	366	117	238	79	120
491		123	114						
721									

COMPUTERS

1	2	3	4	5	6	7	8	9	0
121	42	13	14	25	76	57	18	19	30
151	92	73	24	85	116	97	48	29	40
591		123		235		107		39	

LIBRARIES

1	2	3	4	5	6	7	8	9	0
21	12	33	34	15	16	27	58	49	60
71	22	123	54	55	156	47	78	99	90
	82		114	255		87	108	119	110
						117			

Each index card contains the accession numbers of documents that deal in some way with that concept. These are usually arranged in ten columns according to the final digit of the accession number, as illustrated above.

Now suppose we receive a request for documents about *'Computers in libraries'*. We would retrieve the term cards headed *Computers* and *Libraries* from the file. These are then examined for accession numbers that are *common to both of them*. In our example document number *123* is common to both and therefore this document should contain information on *both elementary concepts* constituting the compound. This document should, therefore, contain information relevant to the compound subject itself—*'Computers in libraries'*.

We have thus achieved a *coordination* of the two concepts constituting the compound class *Computers in libraries*.

At what stage has this coordination of concepts taken place?

At the indexing stage — frame 354

At the search stage — frame 356

You think that post-coordinate indexing will usually include the translation stage of indexing. This is right.

Whenever we use an *indexing language,* and this is common practice in post-coordinate indexing, we must *translate* into the terms used by that language.

Post-coordinate, like pre-coordinate, indexing thus involves
1) a conceptual or subject analysis of the document;
2) translation of this subject analysis into the terms of the particular indexing language in use.

A post-coordinate indexing language consists basically of a set of terms which have been selected for use as indexing terms or subject descriptors.

These terms are arranged, almost invariably, in A/Z order.

In essence these indexing languages are very similar to the lists of subject headings (eg Sear's and Library of Congress) which are used in pre-coordinate indexing. The basic difference is that a post-coordinate indexing language employs only a very limited degree of pre-coordination of terms. The indexing terms are mostly isolate concepts and are not in the form of compound subject headings.

Such a post-coordinate indexing language is usually called a *THESAU-RUS.* This name is derived from Roget's use of the term and there is often little justification for its application to post-coordinate indexing languages.

A true thesaurus incorporates a *classified* arrangement of concepts as well as an A/Z list. An excellent example of such a thesaurus is the *Thesaurofacet: a thesaurus and faceted classification for engineering and related subjects.* Developed from an existing faceted classification, this was first published as a thesaurus/classification by the English Electric Company in 1969.

However, many thesauri are straightforward alphabetical listings of indexing terms without classified sections.

Following accepted practice, we shall use the term thesaurus to mean *any* post-coordinate indexing language.

Probably the most obvious function of a thesaurus is to control the use of *synonyms* and *word forms* (eg variant spellings, word endings) in the selection of preferred indexing terms.

The directions usually employed are   UF (= use for)
and   *Use*

Thus, if the decision has been made to use the term *Males* instead of the term *Men* in the indexing of documents, the following instructions will be found in the thesaurus

MALES
   UF Men
MEN *use*
MALES

Suppose that the following instructions appeared in a thesaurus
COORDINATE INDEXING
  UF Post-coordinate indexing
POST-COORDINATE INDEXING *use*
COORDINATE INDEXING
What is the preferred indexing term?
Post-coordinate indexing   − frame 361
Coordinate indexing   − frame 365

---

371 (357)
Your answer: WHEAT
         NT Harvesting
No. You would not expect to find this entry in a thesaurus.

The direction NT (Narrower Term) indicates that Harvesting is a narrower term than Wheat.

We said that NT indicates terms that are lower in the generic hierarchy, ie related in the genus/species relationship.

Harvesting is *not* a species of the genus Wheat and therefore the relationship between these terms should *not* be indicated by the direction NT.

Please return to frame 357. Read through the text once more then consider the question carefully and select another answer.

---

372 (368)
RECALL IN POST-COORDINATE INDEXING

The value of having the *relationships* between indexing terms displayed in a thesaurus can be illustrated by considering a search through a Uniterm index for information about a particular compound subject.

Suppose we are searching for information about the subject *'The use of television in remedial teaching in primary schools'*.

Our search prescription is,
    Television x Remedial teaching x Primary schools
However, the number of documents retrieved as a result of this first coordination of terms is insufficient to meet the needs of the user. There is a need to *increase recall.*

An increase in recall can be achieved by *broadening the search.*

One way of broadening the search is by *dropping concepts* from the *search prescription.* In doing this we *increase the area of intersection* or broaden the class of documents being searched.

This can be illustrated by the following diagrams.

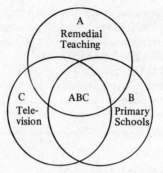

Diagram 1: Search Prescription: Television x Remedial Teaching x Primary Schools

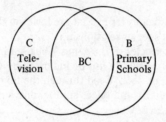

Diagram 2: Search Prescription: Television x Primary Schools

In diagram 1 we have the search prescription *Television x Remedial Teaching x Primary Schools.* The class of documents that we are thus searching is that represented by the area of intersection *ABC*.

In diagram 2 we have the search prescription *Television x Primary Schools.* We have thus *dropped* the concept *Remedial Teaching* from the search prescription.

The class of documents that we are searching has thus been broadened and is diagramatically represented by the area of intersection *BC*.

GENERIC SEARCH

Another method of widening the area of search is to *broaden each concept individually.*

For example, the concept Primary Schools is *included* within the wider class Schools, as illustrated in the following diagram.

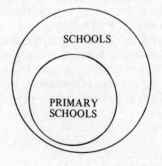

If we search the concept Schools instead of Primary Schools we thus broaden the class of documents being searched. This broadening of the search has been achieved by examining a term of a *higher generic level.* We are now searching the *genus* Schools instead of one *species* of this genus, Primary Schools. Because we have utilized the *generic hierarchy,* ie moved up the generic hierarchy in order to broaden the search, this is called a *generic search.* Thus, if our initial search prescription *Television x Remedial teaching x Primary Schools* yields insufficient documents, we can search at a higher generic level by using the search prescription.

    Television x Remedial teaching x Schools

This, of course, assumes that we consider the concept Primary Schools to be the inhibiting factor in the initial search.

In this instance we have broadened the search by simply substituting a genus for one of its species in the search prescription.

Most of the *additional* documents retrieved, ie those indexed under the genus and not the species, will presumably deal with the subject in question at a more general level.

We can even more effectively increase recall by conducting a generic search in which we substitute the unsatisfactory term by its *genus and other species of that genus* in addition to the particular one we are concerned with.

    eg   *Television x Remedial teaching x (Schools + Infant schools + Primary schools + Secondary schools).*

By this means we not only retrieve documents of a more general nature but also documents dealing with various specific terms that supplement our knowledge of the subject we are interested in.

Which of the following broadens most effectively an unsatisfactory search for *Objectives x Suburban* Youth through the conducting of a generic search?

Objectives x (Suburban youth + Urban youth
+ Rural youth + Immigrant youth)   – frame 380
Objectives x Youth   – frame 366
Objectives x (Suburban youth + Urban youth
+ Rural youth + Immigrant youth + Youth)   – frame 375

---

373 (374)

You say that you would *reject* the document indexed

    Programmed Instruction[3] Vocational education[3]

No, you would not.

The weighting 3 indicated that this document provides *significant treatment* of the concepts Programmed Instruction and Vocational Education.

In rejecting it you are failing to fulfil the user's request adequately.

Please return to frame 374. Read about weighting again, then consider the question carefully, select the correct answer, and continue the course.

Correct. By assigning an index description in the pre-coordinated form
Student Opinion we ensure that this document will only be retrieved in
response to a request for information about *'The opinions of students'*.
If we used the two isolate concepts Students *and* Opinions confusion
might arise in that it would appear potentially relevant to requests for
information about opinions *towards* students.

Pre-coordination of indexing terms is particularly suitable for *frequently
occurring compounds* in the literature of any given subject. In such cases,
eg Television advertising in the literature of advertising, coordination at
the search stage is unnecessarily wasteful of time.

WEIGHTING

The devices mentioned so far indicate in some way the relationships
between concepts in documents.

Another device employed at the indexing stage is *weighting*. This
improves precision by indicating the *relative importance* of a concept
within a document.

If we indicate which are major and which are minor concepts within
a document, then we are able to retrieve, when necessary, only those
documents in which the subject of the search is treated as a major concept. We can thus reject documents which have only a small amount of
information about the subject requested.

In this way we improve precision.

Let us presume a *scale of weighting* 1, 2 and 3.

In this scale 3 indicates a concept of *major significance*. 2 and 1 indicate concepts of *decreasing significance*, 1 indicating concepts of *least
importance*.

Suppose you have a request for information about *'Programmed instruction in vocational education'*. The user only requires documents in
which this subject receives significant treatment.

Which of the documents indexed in the following ways would you
reject as containing insufficient relevant information?

Programmed instruction[1] Vocational education[1] — frame 381
Programmed instruction[3] Vocational education[3] — frame 373

375 (372)
Your answer: Objectives x (Suburban youth + Urban youth +
Rural youth + Immigrant youth + Youth).
Correct. This is the most effective generic search as it increases recall by
adding the genus and a selection of the species of that genus including
the one we are especially interested in.

NON-GENERIC SEARCH

Sometimes it is difficult to ask for *generically related terms* and, instead,
we must broaden the search by using *non-generically related terms*. These
may be properties, processes, agents etc of the *unsatisfactory term*. As
such they should be listed in a thesaurus under the comprehensive direction *Related Terms* (RT).

For example, if a search for *Anxiety x Academic achievement* does
not retrieve enough material we may alter (broaden) the search to

Anxiety x (Academic achievement + Gifted + High achievers)

The search is thus broadened even though the added terms are not
kinds of *academic achievement*. Gifted and High achievers are related
terms to Academic achievement in that Academic achievement is a *Property*
of the gifted and the high achiever.

Whether we increase recall through conducting generic or non-generic
searches, the value of having relationships between indexing terms conveniently displayed in a thesaurus is obvious. They help guide the
searcher in the planning and modification of search prescriptions.

Please continue on the next frame.

PRECISION IN POST-COORDINATE INDEXING

We have looked briefly at some of the ways in which recall can be improved in the searching of systems employing post-coordinate indexing.

In Section 2 of this course we saw that recall is increased if the depth of indexing is increased — a greater degree of exhaustivity in indexing leads to a higher recall in searching.

We also noted in Section 2 that an increase in recall tends to have an adverse effect on another measure of performance, precision — as recall is increased precision is lowered.

If a system employing post-coordinate indexing follows a policy of indexing in depth then it will possess an in-built tendency to produce high recall and, consequently, precision will be lowered.

It is true that post-coordinate indexing lends itself well to a depth indexing policy, to the statement of sub-themes in documents in addition to the main theme. It would, however, be misleading to think that a high degree of depth indexing is *always* characteristic of post-coordinate indexing. It is very possible that, in many situations, post-coordinate systems will aim at no greater depth of indexing than pre-coordinate indexing systems.

Irrespective of the depth of indexing, however, the essential simplicity of post-coordinate indexing is a factor that can lead to a lowering of precision at the search stage.

In pre-coordinate indexing a decision must be made as to which concept is *subordinated* to another. This decision calls for a consideration of the *relationships* between categories implicit in a *citation order.*

In post-coordinate indexing, as described so far, the relationships between the constituent concepts of a compound subject are usually *ignored* at the indexing stage.

Simplicity gained by ignoring these relationships at the indexing stage can lead to the retrieval of irrelevant information (ie documents) at the search stage.

Continue on the next frame

Suppose you have a document which has as one of its themes the *television advertising of cosmetics* and, as another, *the press advertising of furniture.*

If this is document number twenty-five in the collection it will receive the following Uniterm index entries. (Of course other document numbers would appear on the ten column cards).

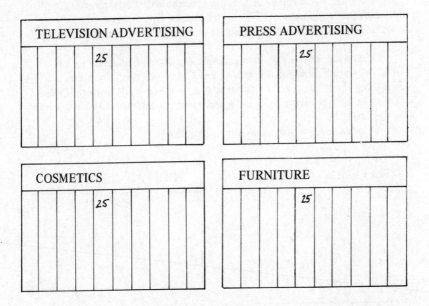

Now, if a request is placed for information about the *television advertising of furniture* a search through the Uniterm index would retrieve document number twenty-five even though it does *not* deal with this subject.

This is an example of a *false drop* — a non-relevant document retrieved because of a weakness in the indexing system. Such failings are also said to give rise to 'noise' in a retrieval system.

Continue on the next frame

Such false drops occur in post-coordinate indexing systems when the *relationships* between concepts treated in documents are not shown. To help eliminate false drops, and thereby *improve precision*, certain *devices* can be employed at the *indexing stage*. These are called *precision devices.*

Links

The device known as *links* (sometimes referred to as 'interfixing') simply indicates that *some* connection exists between two or more terms (ie concepts) in a particular document. The exact nature of this connection is not stated.

For instance, in our previous example drawn from advertising, the *'link'* between *Television advertising* and *Cosmetics* could be indicated by adding the letter A to the document number on each Uniterm index card. The link between *Press advertising* and *Furniture* could be indicated by the letter B.

The index cards would now appear as follows.

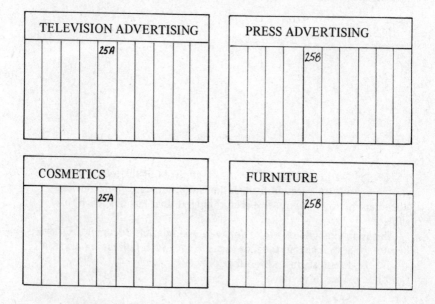

If a search for information about *'Television advertising of furniture'* were now made document number twenty-five would be rejected as non-relevant.

The links between the concepts Television advertising and Furniture do not agree in respect of this document.

The use of links thus indicates that certain concepts within a document are linked to form a *theme* within that document.

This amounts to the same thing as summarization. We are not summarizing the total content of a document but we are summarizing certain *themes* within it.

Instead of simply saying that a document deals with concepts 1, 2, 3 and 4 as *isolated concepts,* we indicate that it deals with, say, concepts *1 and 2* as a theme and concepts *3 and 4* linked as a theme.

Roles

These are indicators assigned by the indexer to particular terms in order to show the exact *role* or function which that term performs in a given document.

For example, if a document about *'The attitudes of students towards teachers'* were indexed simply by assigning it the terms Attitudes, Students and Teachers it would be retrieved in response to a request for information about the very different subject *'The attitudes of teachers towards students'.*

In this instance links would be insufficient to eradicate the false drop. Simple linking of Students and Attitudes would still not make it clear whether it was the attitudes *of* or *towards* Students.

We must indicate more precisely the relations between the terms by indicating their roles within the document.

The use of roles thus assigns individual concepts into various broad *categories* of concept.

In the above case we need to show that Students belongs to say the *Active* Category and Teachers to the *Passive* category.

If our document is number thirty in the collection then Uniterm index cards upon which *role indicators* are used might appear as follows.

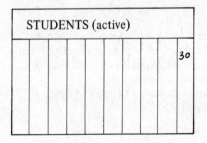

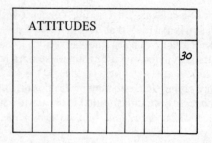

ATTITUDES

30

The search programme would use the same system of role indicators as the indexing and so a request for *'Students' attitudes to teachers'* would have the search prescription

'Students (active) x Attitudes x Teachers (passive)

In this way a false drop is avoided and precision is improved.

Continue on the next frame

---

379 (378)

PRE-COORDINATION IN POST-COORDINATE INDEXING

The use of links and roles improves precision by indicating the *relationships* between concepts *at the indexing stage of a document.*

In doing this, ie indicating relationships at the indexing stage, we introduce an element characteristic of *pre-coordinate indexing.*

Indeed, to improve precision, a certain amount of *coordination of terms* at the *indexing stage* may well be employed. This will indicate their relationships just as in pre-coordinate indexing.

For example, if we have a document about *'Teachers' attitudes'* we might well index this by the pre-coordinated, compound term

Teachers' attitudes

This pre-coordination improves precision by narrowing the search and eliminating documents that include these two concepts, Teachers and Attitudes, in other and possibly irrelevant ways, eg Attitudes *towards* Teachers.

A document deals with the *opinions of students.*

Which of the following index descriptions would ensure the greatest precision in the retrieval of this document?

   1 Students
      Opinions   – frame 367
   2 Student Opinion – frame 374

380 (372)
Your answer: Objectives x (Suburban youth + Urban youth + Rural youth + Immigrant youth).

You are almost right. You have broadened the search by including other species but you have not also included the genus.

Please return to frame 372. Reconsider the question carefully. Select the correct answer and proceed with the course.

---

381 (374)
You say that the document indexed Programmed instruction[1] Vocational education[1] would be rejected.

Correct. The weighting[1] indicates that the concepts Vocational education and Programmed instruction are relatively minor sub-themes within this particular document. The document would therefore not be retrieved as it contains too little information of potential relevance to the request.

The use of such precision devices as weighting, links and roles obviously adds to the effort involved in indexing — and therefore to time and expense. Such factors would need to be borne in mind when considering the value of increased precision. Moreover, although a simple Uniterm system is suitable for the employment of such devices they are not equally easily applicable to all physical forms of post-coordinate indexes. Weighting, for example, if used, is most often done so in computer-based retrieval systems.

SUMMARY

1 In pre-coordinate indexing compound subjects are indexed as compound subjects—coordination of concepts takes place at the indexing stage.

2 This involves citation order decisions and the subordination of concepts, one to another, in compound descriptions.

3 Such decisions give rise to the problem of providing access to the subordinated concepts.

4 Traditional pre-coordinate indexes attempt to overcome this central problem in a variety of ways in both single specific and multiple specific entry systems.

5 Post-coordinate indexing offers another approach to dealing with compound subjects.

6 In essence this is to ignore citation order decisions at the indexing stage. Compound subjects are not indexed as compound subjects but are indexed according to their individual constituent concepts.

7 It is at this search stage that co-ordination of the constituent concepts of compound subjects take place.

8 This approach has given rise to particular kinds of indexing languages, thesauri, and particular forms of index.

9 The essential simplicity of this approach can lead to lowered precision.

10 Certain devices, eg links, roles and weighting, can be employed at the indexing stage to help counterbalance this factor.

11 Such devices introduce into post-coordinate indexing some of the inherent features of pre-coordinate indexing, eg the indication of relationships between concepts at the indexing stage—indeed the use of pre-coordinate descriptors is to be found to varying degrees in post-coordinate systems.

Continue on the next frame

---

382 (381)

In this final section of the course, now completed, we have looked at some of the fundamental characteristics of post-coordinate indexing and the ways in which it differs from pre-coordination. In the illustration of these characteristics we have referred to only one physical form of index, the Uniterm index. Our interest has lain with indexing practices rather than with search procedures and to this extent we have excluded consideration of different physical types of index as not materially affecting the basic principles of indexing.

However, it is clear that the mechanics of searching post-coordinate indexes differ from those involved in searching conventional, pre-coordinate indexes. The former necessitate the constant comparison, or manipulation, of index entries rather than the linear scanning of entries in the latter.

Over the years different kinds of indexes have been developed to facilitate this activity of comparison in searching. Optical coincidence and edge-notched card systems are examples of such indexes. These types of manual system, although possibly less restrictive than Uniterm, are still basically limited in use to the indexing and searching of relatively small collections of documents.

Post-coordinate indexing is now increasingly associated with computer-based information retrieval systems; the potential search facilities of such systems are well suited to this kind of indexing. The use of the computer in information retrieval is, of course, not only related to coordinate indexing. Its impact has been, and continues to be, extremely far reaching, having relevance to all the areas we have covered in a variety of ways. We have excluded consideration of the many applications of the computer in pre- and post-coordinate indexing as lying beyond the limits and objectives of this particular course.

What we have tried to do is to introduce some of the underlying principles of subject indexing with reference to traditional forms of index. These principles are being applied in an ever increasing variety of contexts, both manual and automated. It is our contention that an understanding of such basic principles is fundamental to an appreciation of these many and varied contexts, and their products, that the individual is likely to encounter. We hope that you have found this course of some help in increasing that understanding on your part.

COLON CLASSIFICATION: Categories and citation order in 6th ed
(Classes arranged in UDC order for comparison and aid in using UDC)

UDC	Class	CC	Canonical divisions	Systems	Specials	P₁	P₂	P₃	P₄	M	E	2P	2P₂	2E	3P
02	Library science	2				Libraries				Stock	Operations				
1	Philosophy	R	Logics, Ethics, etc												
159.9	Psychology	S		Gestalt		Persons					Mental processes				Anatomy, Pathology, etc
2	Religion	Q				Religions					Beliefs and practices				
248.2	Mysticism	△				Religions	God, Devil, Man, etc				Techniques				
30	Sociology	Y				Groups					Activities			Treatment of social problems	
311	Statistics	B28													
32	Political science	W				Form of state	Offices of state				Practices, policies, and problems				
33+38 & 65	Economics	X		Communism, etc	Scale	Business					Activities				
34	Law	Z				Legal system	Subjects of law								
35	Public administration		This subject distributed in Colon classes V, X, M and L												

UDC	Class	CC	Canunical divisions	Systems	Specials	P₁	P₂	P₃	P₄	M	E	2P	2P₂	2E	3P
36	Social work	YX	No schedule given in Colon. Assume similar structure to Y												
37	Education			Montessori, etc		Stages						Activities	Subject taught / Methods and taught aids	Treatment of social problems	
39	Social anthropology	Y7				Groups					Activities				
4	Linguistics	P				Language variants	Stage elements				Structure and analysis				
502	Natural history		This subject distributed in Colon at G:12, I:12, K:12.												
51	Mathematics	B	Arithmetic, algebra, etc			Differential treatment within canonical divisions									
52	Astronomy	B9				Heavenly body					Orbits, eclipses, etc				
53	Physics	C	Heat, Light, etc			Differential treatment within canonical divisions									
531/533	Mechanics	B7				State of matter					Process				
54	Chemistry	H1				Substance					Process				
548	Mineralogy	H				Substance					Operations				
55	Earth sciences (Geology, etc)	H	Petrology, etc			Differential treatment within canonical divisions									
56	Paleontology	H6				Fossils									
571	Archaeology	V:71	(distributed class by country)												

APPENDIX (continued)

UDC	Class	CC	Canonical divisions	Systems	Specials	P₁	P₂	P₃	P₄	M	E	2P	2P₂	2E	3P
572	Physical anthropology	Y7:2				Race									
574	Biology	G			Stage of growth	Organ					Processes				
58	Botany	I				Plant	Organ				Processes				
59	Zoology	K				Animal	Organ				Processes				
61	Medicine	L		Homeopathy, etc	Stage of growth, etc	Organ					Processes			Treatment of diseases	Treatment of diseases
62	Engineering	D				Civil, Mechanical, etc	Part			Material	Operations				
622	Mining	HX				Substance	Plant and equipment								
63	Agriculture	J		Forestry, etc	Soilless farming, etc	Crop	Organ				Operations				
636/639	Animal husbandry	KX				Animal					Operations			Treatment of diseases, etc	
64	Domestic	MA				Cooking, etc					Operations			Treatment of diseases, etc	
66/67	Chemical technology	F				Product					Operations				
67/68	Useful arts	M	Various crafts			Product					Operations				

UDC	Class	CC	Canonical divisions	Systems	Specials	P₁	P₂	P₃	P₄	M	E	2P	2P₂	2E	3P
69	Building	D3				Kind of build-ing	Part of building			Material	Operations				
7	Fine arts	N	Various arts			Style ———— (for all arts)									
71	Town planning	NB				"	"	Kind of town	Part of town		Operations				
72	Architecture	NA				"	"	Kind of building	Part of building		Operations				
73/76	Sculpture, painting, etc	ND, etc				"	"	Subject		Material	Operations				
77	Photography	M95													
78	Music	NR				Style		Form etc		Instruments	Technique				
791/795	Entertainment (drama, cinema, etc)	NS/NW													
796/799	Sports	MY				Various sports									
8	Literature	O				Lan-guage	Form	Author	Work		Criticism				
91	Geography	U				Physical, economic, etc									
92	Biography	W				Coun-try	Offices of state				Activities				
93	History	V													

INDEX

The frame numbers given indicate where a concept is first introduced.
When appropriate, a subsequent treatment of the concept is also indicated.